DIS

THE TOWER SERIES OF ANGLO-IRISH STUDIES I

GENERAL EDITOR ROGER MC HUGH

THE CELTIC TWILIGHT AND THE NINETIES

AUSTIN CLARKE

The Celtic Twilight
and the Nineties

with an introduction by
ROGER MC HUGH

THE TOWER SERIES
OF ANGLO-IRISH STUDIES I

DUFOUR EDITIONS

*Set in Times Roman type with Pilgrim display, and
printed and published in the Republic of Ireland at the
Dolmen Press, 8 Herbert Place, Dublin 2.*

1970

*Distributed outside Ireland, except in the U.S.A. and
Canada by Oxford University Press
and in the U.S.A. and Canada by Dufour Editions Inc.,
Chester Springs, Pennsylvania, 19425.*

Contents

Foreword

In 1965 I had the pleasure of inviting Austin Clarke to give a series of talks at University College, Dublin, with the understanding that they should be published subsequently. The result is this volume, the first in the new Tower Series associated with our School of Anglo-Irish studies.

As a young poet Austin Clarke experienced the literary aftermath of the Nineties and of the Victorians and came to know Yeats shortly after his emergence from his Celtic Twilight period. Clarke's early poetry, while sharing Yeats's interest in early Irish literature, followed an independent line of development, while his own verse-drama, which has reached a stature at least comparable with that of Yeats, was born partly of reaction against Yeats's attitude to the theatre. During the past thirty years Clarke's productions for radio and stage of verse-plays, including those of Yeats, have been largely responsible for keeping poetic drama alive in Ireland during a time when it has been neglected by the Abbey Theatre. He has also played an important part in helping the work of the Lyric Theatre, Belfast.

These circumstances, coupled with his wide knowledge of English and continental traditions in poetry and poetic drama and with an acute and sometimes acrid critical sense, make Austin Clarke a unique commentator upon the literature and environment which he discusses in these pages.

ROGER MC HUGH
General Editor.
University College, Dublin.

The Nineties

T O   M O S T   P E O P L E , the words, 'the 1890's' mean the
Fin de Siècle movement, abroad and in England. Indeed
the very use of the French phrase indicates that the movement as such was exotic; in fact, not quite English and,
therefore, shocking. Actually the last decade of the nineteenth century was an extraordinarily varied period, full of
all sorts of movements and counter-movements, new and
old influences. One feels at times as if one were at a
crowded railway junction with trains arriving and depart-
ing from various platforms. Some writers felt that a great
epoch was ending and turned either to the passing moment
or the romantic past; others, however, like H. G. Wells,
G. B. Shaw, felt that everything was only beginning and
looked forward, with an optimism which has been much
disturbed since then, to the dazzling progress of a new
century. Most of the poets, such as Ernest Dowson, Lionel
Johnson, Richard le Gallienne, Arthur Symons—and we
must include W. B. Yeats—looked back to the romantic
period, feeling that they were in the twilight of the ages.
We can now see that they were in a minority and they
themselves really knew it for they were opposed to Naturalism, the intensely realistic movement, led by Zola, which
had been spreading from the seventies, and was introduced
into English by George Moore. In his Introduction to *The
Eighteen-Nineties*, an anthology of the Decadence, chosen
by Martin Secker, Mr. John Betjeman has given us the
following pleasant recipe:
> 'Draw the curtains, kindle a joss-stick in a dark corner,
> settle down on a sofa by the fire, light an Egyptian
> cigarette and sip a brandy and soda, as you think your-
> self back to the world which ended in prison and dis-
> grace for Wilde, suicide for Crackenthorpe and John
> Davidson, premature death for Beardsley, Dowson,
> Lionel Johnson, religion for some, drink and drugs for

others, temporary or permanent oblivion for many more.'

That passage may seem rather frivolous but there is an element of sound criticism in it. When the prevailing mood is one of languour, world-weariness, despair, we cannot take it too seriously for we have to consider the problem of literary fashion. Certainly the movement ended abruptly with the coming of the twentieth century. The long interval of peace was over; the British Empire was fighting the Boers, and Kipling was the poet of war and conquest. Most of the young writers of the nineties were already dead; those who survived were quickly forgotten. W. B. Yeats and George Moore returned promptly to Dublin to hasten on the Irish Literary Revival.

Academic critics still regard severely the movement of the nineties but there has always been a popular interest in it. As a student, I was first attracted to it by Holbrook Jackson's sympathetic study entitled *The Eighteen-Nineties*, and it seemed to me , as I read about it, a remote period. When I settled down in London in my early twenties, I was to realise during my first week there that the nineties were not so distant. One afternoon, I left the Six Bells in Chelsea, where I had been drinking mild-and-bitter with an acquaintance, and went with him to an Exhibition given by a young Scottish artist of the modern school. In his paintings he used only the colours of the spectrum. As I moved slowly among the crowd, the red, orange, yellow, green, blue, indigo of cubes were confused blurs for I was not used to English beer. In a far corner I was introduced to the elderly Comtesse de Bremont, an American lady, who had written a volume of reminiscences. She talked to me of her old friend, Oscar Wilde: and I forgot at once the anecdotes which she related to me. Three weeks later, I was shocked to read in the newspaper that she had been found dead in her lodgings and, according to the coroner, her death was due to malnutrition. I could not help thinking again of the tragic fate of the other writers of the nineties.

10

Soon afterwards I was invited to the basement kitchen of a flat in Earls Court, where a group of little-known poets met once a month to read their verse to one another. Most of the poems I heard were indifferent and, being young and confident, I was certain that I would make an impression. But the two lyrics which I read out were received without comment and, in dejection I went back to my warm place near the closed range. Tea was served and amid the general conversation I sat alone. Suddenly a small dapper man with a cravat and monocle came over to me and, with a slight bow, said, 'I am Victor Plarr', and complimented me on my poems. I was astonished for I had believed that he was long since dead. I had read his short biography of his friend, Ernest Dowson, and admired his epigrammatic lines about Mabel Beardsley, the sister of the famous artist.

Stand not uttering sedately
Trite oblivious praise about her!
Rather say you saw her lately
Lightly kissing her last lover.

Whisper not 'There is a reason
Why we bring her no white blossom:'
Since the snowy bloom's in season,
Strow it on her sleeping bosom:

Oh, for it would be a pity
To o'erpraise her or to flout her:
She was wild, and sweet, and witty—
Let's not say dull things about her.

Yeats, if I am right, owed something to this poem many years later when he wrote his own poem about Mabel Beardsley entitled 'Upon a Dying Lady'.

Some time later, I met George Egerton, an Irish writer, who won international fame during the nineties and then had been forgotten. Like George Sands and George Eliot, she had chosen a male pseudonym: her real name was Mary Dunne. She had belonged to the modernistic movement and wrote her first collection of short stories during an inspired summer in Mill Street, Co. Cork. *Keynotes* was published by John Lane in 1894 and the title page design was by Aubrey Beardsley. The international vogue of George Egerton can easily be understood for her themes were sophisticated and their milieu was cosmopolitan: Norway, London, Paris, Holland, Ireland. Moreover these short stories were psychological studies, experiments in a free form, which had rid itself of the exigencies and falsifying tendencies of plot. They revealed the New Woman, not yet content to abandon mystery, charm, or even naughtiness, and, appropriately, their style was witty, incisive and yet lyrical, when necessary, in mood. In one of her stories about Dublin, she gave us a first glimpse of Night Town long before it was described by James Joyce in *Ulysses*. She had met Ibsen, lived with Knut Hamsun and knew the other young Norwegian writers. Like many others, she had become converted to the cause of Irish independence by the events of the Rising. She gave me a collection of short stories by the composer Arnold Bax, who had lived for some years in Ireland and wrote under the pen-name Dermot O'Byrne. From her, too, I heard for the first time of that great story by Seamus O'Kelly, *The Weaver's Grave*. Her new interest in Irish literature proved an inspiration and she wrote a group of stories about this country but they have never been published. One of them which I remember very well is now topical in interest for it deals with the colour problem. A young Negro in the West Indies, a descendant of one of the Irish rebels sold into slavery in the Barbadoes during the Cromwellian period, was so stirred by the Rising that he saved up sufficient money to visit the land of his father's ancestors. On his first day in Cork, he went into a public house on the Coal Quay and got into conversation with some labourers who were drinking pints of Beamish there. They were flattered by his knowledge of the happenings of Easter Week. 'What's your name?' one of them asked. 'Patrick

12

Jeremiah O'Sullivan,' he replied proudly. Believing that he was having a joke at their expense, the enraged workmen threw the unfortunate black man out into the street.

We can trace back the *Fin de Siècle* movement on the Continent to the late eighties. George Rodenbach, who died of consumption in 1898, was the first, as far as I know, to evoke the melancholy twilight mood. He depicted the quiet, swan-reflecting canals of his native city, Bruges, its old houses, its side-streets and alms-houses in delicate impressionistic lyrics, and won celebrity with his novel, *Bruges la Morte*, much to the annoyance of his fellow townsmen, who were more interested in the coming age of Industrialism. Rodenbach was one of the first of the modern Symbolists, although he is not mentioned in Edmund Wilson's well-known study of symbolism, *Axel's Castle*. He was succeeded by Maurice Maeterlinck, who explored what we might call the dimmer states of mind and its intimations. He writes of lonely castles in remote forests, princesses pining in towers or dungeons, each princess being a symbol or aspect of the soul. But even when expressing vague langourous moods, Maeterlinck can at the same time use an unusual kind of imagery, which is modern and analytic in its sharpness. Here is one of his poems, in which he is trying to define the paradoxical fancies in the delirium of fever. It is entitled 'The Hospital'.

> Hospital! Hospital on the canal!
> Hospital in July!
> There is a fire in the room!
> While ocean liners blow their sirens on the canal!
>
> (O! do not come near the windows!)
> Emigrants are crossing a palace!
> I see a yacht in the tempest!
> I see flocks on all the ships!
> (It is better to keep all the windows closed,
> One is almost sheltered from the outside.)
> It is like a hothouse on snow,

13

You are going to a woman's churching on a stormy day,
You have a glimpse of plants shed over a linen sheet,
There is a conflagration in the sun,
And I cross a forest full of wounded men.

O! now at last the moonlight!

A jet of water rises in the middle of the room!
A troop of little girls half open the door!

I catch a glimpse of lambs on an island in the meadows!
And of beautiful plants on a glacier!
And lilies in a marble vestibule!
There is a festival in a virgin forest!
And an oriental vegetation in a cave of ice!

Listen! the locks are opened!
And the ocean liners stir the water of the canal!

O! but the sister of charity poking the fire!

And all the beautiful green rushes of the banks are on fire!
A vessel full of wounded men rocks in the moonlight!
All the King's daughters are in a bark in the storm!
And the Princesses are going to die in a field of hemlock!

O! do not leave the lattices open!
Listen! the ocean liners still are blowing their sirens on the horizon!

Someone is being poisoned in a garden!
People are banqueting in the house of their enemies!
There are stags in a town that is being besieged!
And a menagerie among the lilies!
There is tropical vegetation in a coal-pit!
A flock of sheep is crossing an iron bridge!
And the lambs of the meadows are coming sadly into the room!

Now the sister of charity lights the lamps,
She brings the patients their supper,
She has closed the windows on the canal,
And all the doors to the moon.

Maeterlinck became interested in scientific exploration
and combined imagination and observation in a highly
individual way, as in his *Life of the Bee*. He won fame by
his plays and essays but in recent years his reputation has
declined.

Verlaine, who had much influence, was master of the
hint, the nuance and of a delicate and evasive rhythm: his
lyrical method has much in common with that of the Impressionistic painters. In his poem, *Art Poetique*, he sums
up his attitude in a famous first line—

De la musique avant toute chose.

and every stanza begins with a definition of the new art—

Car nous voulons la Nuance encore,
Pas la Couleur, rien que la nuance!

A young contemporary of his, Albert Samain, expressed the
same new ideal, an ideal which many regarded as decadent.
Here are some lines of Samain translated by the American
poet, Amy Lowell:

I dream of soft verses and intimate branchings and
entwinings,
Of verses which brush against the soul like wings.

Of pale-hued verses, whose fluid meaning streams
wide,
As under the water streams Ophelia's hair.

Of silent verses, without rhythm and without plot,
Where the noiseless rhyme slips past like an oar.

Of verses of an ancient stuff, exhausted,
Impalpable like sound and cloud.

Of verses of Autumn evenings, enchanting the hours
With the feminine rite of minor syllables.

The Fin de Siècle is also known as the Decadent Movement, the Aesthetic Movement and, of course, the Naughty Nineties, the latter being apt in its alliteration. It also has been called the Yellow Book period for that famous periodical, *The Yellow Book,* had yellow covers, associated in the public mind with wicked French novels. In that fine book, *The Romantic Agony,* Professor Mario Praz traces the great romantic movement of Europe to its gradual decline towards the end of the nineteenth century. Apart from immediate Continental influences, the English poets of the last decade had their own tradition, which derives from the pre-Raphaelite poets, Rossetti, Swinburne, William Morris. Swinburne, with his extraordinary mastery of musical metres, had appeared suddenly in the 'sixties and his influence was to prove immense. His famous, or rather notorious, collection, *Poems and Ballads,* published in 1866, proved a startling event because its learned eroticism derived from Baudelaire and the Marquis de Sade. Rossetti had been unfairly attacked by the Scottish poet, Robert Buchanan, as the leader of the 'Fleshly School of Poetry'; Swinburne was denounced by Viscount Morley in a striking phrase as 'the libidinous leader of a pack of satyrs.' Both in prose and verse, however, the great critical influence of the time was Walter Pater. This quiet university don had revolted against the increasing didacticism of the Victorian age and his doctrine of aestheticism, popularised later in the slogan, Art for Art's Sake, was to create a tremendous stir, especially when it was taken up and preached by Oscar Wilde. In order really to understand the second phase of romantic revolt in an age of industrialism, we have to read Pater's two books, his studies in the *History of the Renaissance,* published in the 'seventies, and *Appreciations,* which appeared in the 'eighties. Pater based his precepts on the practice of Flaubert and Gautier. His choice pages are full of memorable definitions. Here is one of them:

'The literary artist is of necessity a scholar, and in what he proposes to do will have in mind, first of all, the

16

scholar and the scholarly conscience.'

And he adds:

'The material in which he works is no more a creation of his own than the sculptor's marble. Product of a myriad various minds and contending tongues, compact of obscure and minute association, a language has its own abundant and often recondite laws, in the habitual and summary recognition of which a scholarship consists. A writer, full of matter he is before all things anxious to express, may think of those laws, the limitation of vocabulary, structure, and the like, as a restriction, but if a real artist will find in them an opportunity.'

Pater was opposed to the otiose, the facile. His ideal was a severe beauty:

'For in truth all art but does consist in the removal of surplusage, from the last finish of the gem-engraver blowing away the last particle of invisible dust, back to the earliest divination of the finished work to be, lying somewhere, according to Michaelangelo's fancy, in the rough-hewn block of stone.'

All this Continental doctrine of art was revolutionary at the time and Pater caused particular offence when he coined the phrase, 'aesthetic poetry' to describe the work of Dante Gabriel Rossetti and William Morris. 'The aesthetic poetry', he wrote, 'is neither mere reproduction of Greek or mediaeval poetry, nor only an idealisation of modern life and sentiment ... Like some strange second flowering after date, it renews on a more delicate type the poetry, of a past age, but must not be confounded with it. The secret of the enjoyment of it is that inversion of home-sickness known to some, that incurable thirst for the sense of escape, which no actual form of life satisfies, no poetry even, if it be merely simple and spontaneous.' There we get for the first time both the definition and the idea of escape. In the 'thirties, 'escapism', as it is called, became a term of abuse, much used by the young political poets in their attack on romantic tradition. The Cambridge

17

History of English Literature has summed up Pater's
doctrine of art for art's sake in a sentence which is just and
at the same time extremely English:

'It sounds an easy solution for life's perplexities, and, as
such, may attract the dilettante and the shirker: but,
taken at its true and intended sense, it is as stern a creed
as religion for religion's sake—a height of devotion to
which few attain.'

Despite Pater's ideal of a severe beauty, the languid and
otiose were to prevail, helped by an extreme musicality. As
early as the 'seventies, Arthur O'Shaughnessy, a poet of
Irish descent, was writing:

We are the music-makers,
And we are the dreamers of dreams,
Wandering by lone sea-breakers,
And sitting by desolate streams;
World-losers and world-forsakers,
On whom the pale moon gleams:
Yet we are the movers and shakers
Of the world forever it seems.

Here, at a second remove, is expressed Baudelaire's idea
of the poet as a social outcast in an age of bourgeois pros-
perity, a theme elaborated by Verlaine in his biographical
studies, *Les Poètes Maudits*. Verlaine was himself one of
these poets who seemed to be accursed. He had been in
gaol for shooting and wounding his fellow-poet, Arthur
Rimbaud, lived a debauched, drunken life and spent a
good deal of it in hospitals. Arthur O'Shaughnessy had
gone on to declare in his lyric:

With wonderful deathless ditties
We build up the world's great cities,
And out of a fabulous story
We fashion an empire's glory.

We have the twentieth answer in T. S. Eliot's well-known
poem, 'The Hollow Men':—

We are the hollow men
We are the stuffed men

18

Leaning together
Headpiece filled with straw. Alas!

Some years ago, a selection from the *Yellow Book* was published in reduced facsimile with drawings by Beardsley, Rothenstein, Walter Crane and even academic artists, including Sir Frederick Leighton. The first thing that struck one was this: that much of the verse was not as good as one had thought it was, but the prose was excellent. Another thing was that the stories and essays in it were not as depraved as one had fancied. There was, for example, an essay on cosmetics by Max Beerbohm, which caused a terrible uproar at the time. Now, when lavish advertisements in every paper proclaim the virtues of lipstick, when ladies powder their noses unashamedly in every restaurant and bus, when indeed all these aids to beauty can be bought in Woolworth's, we can only smile at this daring 'defence of cosmetics.' Indeed cosmetics seem to have been one of the most daring subjects some of these writers could think of. For example, the opening pages of *Under the Hill,* that unfinished erotic prose romance by Aubrey Beardsley, begins with a description of Venus adorning herself before her mirror. It is a delicious piece of artificiality, based on the description of Belinda in Pope's *Rape of the Lock*:

Before a toilet that shone like the altar of Notre Dame des Victoires, Helen was seated in a little dressing-room of black and heliotrope. The coiffeur Cosme was caring for her scented chevalure, and with tiny silver tongs, warm from the caresses of the flame, made delicious intelligent curls that fell as lightly as a breath about her forehead and over her eyebrows, and clustered like tendrils round her neck. Her three favourite girls, Papperlarde, Blanchemains, and Loreyne, waited immediately upon her with perfume and powder in delicate flagons and frail cassolettes, and held in procelain jars the ravishing paints prepared by Chateline for those cheeks and lips that had grown a little pale with anguish and exile. Her three favourite boys, Claud, Clair and Sarrasine,

19

stood amorously about with salver, fan and napkin. Millamant held a slight tray of slippers, Minette some tender gloves, La Popeliniere—mistress of the robes—was ready with a frock of yellow and white, La Zambinella bore the jewels, Florizel some flowers, Amadour a box of various pins, and Vadius a box of sweets. Her doves, ever in attendance, walked about the room that was panelled with the gallant paintings of Jean Baptiste Dorat, and some dwarfs and doubtful creatures sat here and there lolling out their tongues, pinching each other, and behaving oddly enough. Sometimes Helen gave them little smiles.

Ernest Dowson may be regarded as the typical poet type of the nineties. He was born in 1867 and died in 1900 at the age of thirty-three. He led an unhappy bohemian existence and, in a famous couple of sentences, Arthur Symons has described the unhappy love affair which inspired most of his verse.

'The situation seemed to me of the most exquisite and appropriate impossibility. The daughter of a refugee, I believe of good family, reduced to keeping a humble restaurant in a foreign quarter of London, she listened to his verses, smiled charmingly, under her mother's eyes, on his two years' courtship, and at the end of two years married the waiter instead.'

The lyrical poetry of Dowson offers no difficulties. It evokes instantly wistful or melancholy moods, moods of vague regret and world-weariness, but, if I may quote Pater again on aesthetic poetry, 'it is a strange second flowering after date, it renews on a more delicate type the poetry of a past age.' The Latin titles which Dowson affected are significant, for he used those stock images of roses, wine, which come down to us from the Latin poets, Horace, Catullus, Propertius; and from his contemporary, Verlaine, he learned the use of hint, vague association, a delicate broken rhythm. His work is small in bulk but he was the first to master in English the Alexandrine.

20

In English, for some arithmetical reason, the six-foot line breaks into three feet. By delicate variations and pause, transposition of accent, Dowson gave this metre a tantalising quality. We find it in his best-known anthology piece, 'Non sum qualis eram bonae sub Regno Cynarae.' Dowson's resolution of pain and tragedy into remote music is shown, for example, in his poem, 'To One in Bedlam.' The title may seem rather archaic and affected, the diction too poetic. Of course, Bedlam, the old world for madhouse, is a contraction of Bethlehem and so the present and the past in the history of misery are fused.

> With delicate, mad hands, behind his sordid bars,
> Surely he hath his posies, which they tear and twine;
> Those scentless wisps of straw, that miserable line
> His strait, caged universe, whereat the dull world
> stares.

Although Dowson, in his last years, became a Catholic, his religious poems only intensify the literary mood of world-weariness and resignation. The last poem which he wrote, one of only six lines and entitled 'Epigram' shows what seems to be a stronger mood:—

> Because I am idolatrous and have besought,
> With grievous supplication and consuming prayer,
> The admirable image that my dreams have wrought
> Out of her swan's neck and her dark, abundant hair:
> The jealous gods, who brook no worship save their
> own,
> Turned my live idol marble and her heart to stone.

I think we can find something of that cadence in poems which W. B. Yeats was to write in the same measure a decade later.

Lionel Johnson was a friend of Ernest Dowson, Richard Le Gallienne, Yeats and the other poets of the Rhymers' Club, who met in the Cheshire Cheese, an old Fleet Street tavern, now a show-place—not because of the Rhymers, but because Dr. Johnson was supposed to have frequented it. Dowson and Lionel Johnson are the only poets named

21

in the well-known lyric which W. B. Yeats addressed to his 'Companions of the Cheshire Cheese'. Like Dowson, Lionel Johnson was a scholarly poet, but primarily a religious one. At an early age he had become a convert to Catholicism. His classical training gave him his ideal of a lofty eloquence and in another period he probably would have remained a learned aloof writer, but, owing to the romantic mood of the time, he had actually two distinct styles which are kept apart usually in his work. Sometimes they blend: a firm, compact Latin style which reminds us of Marvell; a contemporary one which has all the languour, world-weariness and despair of the rapidly disappearing century. His best poem, perhaps, is 'By the Statue of King Charles at Charing Cross', and here are the opening stanzas:—

Sombre and rich, the skies;
Great glooms, and starry plains.
Gently the night wind sighs;
Else a vast silence reigns.

The splendid silence clings
Around me: and around
The saddest of all kings
Crowned, and again discrowned.

Comely and calm, he rides
Hard by his own Whitehall:
Only the night wind glides:
No crowds, nor rebels, brawl.

Gone, too, his Court: and yet,
The stars his courtiers are:
Stars in their stations set;
And every wandering star.

That scornful reference to the rebels and multitudes is perhaps too deliberate; we become aware of the aristocratic pose, later adopted by Yeats. Though austere in temperament, Johnson led a desperately confused life for he became a victim to drink and died tragically at the com-

paratively early age of thirty-five. He fell backwards from
a high stool at the counter of a Fleet Street public house.
He is the only poet of this group who writes of conscience,
but even his most personal lyrics conceal rather than reveal,
hint rather than define. He was a master of the octosyllabic
measure and used it with delicate variations as in 'The
Dark Angel', which begins: —

Dark Angel, with thine aching lust
To rid the world of penitence:
Malicious Angel, who still dost
My soul such subtle violence!

Because of thee, no thought, no thing,
Abides for me undesecrate:
Dark Angel, ever on the wing,
Who never reaches me too late!

When music sounds, then changest thou
Its silvery to a sultry fire:
Nor will thine envious heart allow
Delight untortured by desire.

Through thee, the gracious Muses turn
To Furies, O mine Enemy!
And all the things of beauty burn
With flame of evil ecstasy.

Here is a short lyric of his in which his two styles are
blended, a lyric which is very much of the nineties: —

I know you, solitary griefs,
Desolate passions, aching hours!
I know you, tremulous beliefs,
Agonised hopes, and ashen flowers!

The winds are sometimes sad to me;
The starry spaces, full of fear:
Mine is the sorrow of the sea,
And mine the sigh of places drear.

Some players upon plaintive strings
Publish their wistfulness abroad:

23

I have not spoken of these things
Save to one man, and unto God.

In talking about the Celtic Twilight, I shall deal with Lionel Johnson's poems about Ireland.

It would be rash, no doubt, to claim too much for this small group of poets who failed to receive due recognition at the time. Nevertheless it is hard to resist the appeal of Yeats's poem on the Last Romantics: —

You had to face your ends when young—
'Twas wine or women, or some curse—
But never made a poorer song
That you might have a heavier purse,
Nor gave loud service in a cause
That you might have a troop of friends,
You kept the Muses' sterner laws,
And unrepenting faced your ends,
And therefore earned the right—and yet
Dowson and Johnson most I praise—
To troop with those the world's forgot,
And copy their proud steady gaze.

There were, of course, other poets in the nineties who did not share the *fin de siècle* mood, Robert Bridges, for example, and Laurence Binyon, but they all had the same problem. Overshadowed by the reputation of Tennyson and Browning, they were forced to seek variations of their own; they had to avoid, if they could, the mellifluous Tennyson line, the brisk conversational rhythm of Browning. This had also been the problem of poets writing in the eighties. W. E. Henley, poet and journalist, tried to bring modern realism into verse, particularly in his Hospital poems, and he experimented in free rhythms. R. L. Stevenson was a stylist but also a lover of fresh air. He proclaimed the joys of the open road and the far horizon. In fact, he might be described as the first hiker. Andrew Lang, Edmund Gosse, Austin Dobson and others were experimenting in the intricate forms of courtly verse, which had been revived in France by Theodore de Banville and the writing of rondeaux, ballades, villanelles became a fashion.

Of the poets of the Rhymers' Club, Richard Le Gallienne was at the time one of the best-known but it is hard to say much for his verse now. His neglected novels, however, are of interest and, being short, they are readable for they conform to the length of the French novel and in some of them the decadent mood reaches its extreme. Here is the opening paragraph of one of them, a neat and amusingly 'precious' description of the sordid background of the Industrial Age:—

On the dreary suburban edge of a very old, very ignorant, very sooty, hard-hearted, stony-streeted, meanly grim, little provincial town there stands a gasometer. On one side of this gasometer begins a region of disappointed fields, which, however, has hardly begun before a railway embankment cuts across, at an angle convenient for its entirely obscuring the few meadows and trees that in this desolate land do duty for a countryside. The dull workmen's streets that here abruptly present unfinished ends to the universe must console themselves with the gasometer. And indeed they seem more than content. For a street boasting the best view, as it runs out its sordid line longer than the rest, is proudly called Gasometer Street.

The American artist, Whistler, one of the outstanding personalities of the nineties, drew attention in his essay, 'The Gentle Art of Making Enemies', to what he called the Cult of the Gasometer. In the twenties of our century, the gasometer became a kind of symbol to the new poets, owing to those lines of T. S. Eliot, which have been so often quoted:—

While I was fishing in the dull canal
On a Winter evening round behind the gashouse
Musing upon the king my brother's wreck
And on the king my father's death before him.

Arthur Symons, another of the Rhymers' Club group, never really achieved a reputation as a poet, but he was a remarkable critic and his influence was extensive. He was always discovering the latest abroad, but his evaluations were often extraordinarily just. He introduced Verlaine to an English public, translated plays of D'Annunzio, wrote a history of the Symbolist Movement. He, too, was a tragic figure for his later years were overshadowed by recurrent fits of insanity.

Alice Meynell was a fastidious writer both in her verse and essays. Her husband and she rescued Francis Thompson from destitution. In his Bohemian helplessness and addiction to drink and drugs, Thompson was very much of the period; imaginatively he drew his inspiration from the great Baroque age of religious art.

In 1896, appeared a small book of poems, which eventually became as popular as Fitzgerald's *Ruba'iyyat of Omar Khayyam*. This was *A Shropshire Lad* and its author later became well known as a considerable Latin scholar. A. E. Housman was really another of the scholar poets defined by Walter Pater, although he concealed this scholarship in his poems. In these he blends a classic sense of form and precision of language with the direct simplicity of the traditional ballad, using the ballad metre most of the time. He achieved a constant variety in it by subtle touches. One set of critics tells us that his poems do not give us a real picture of simple folk: they are the morbid brooding of an introverted young man of the nineties. There is something to be said for this point of view but it is too extreme. These compressed lyrics and short ballads about unhappy Shropshire lads, all fated to be hanged or die fighting in far distant lands, do capture something of common tradition. The penal history of England, as of other countries, is a terrible one: the miseries of the poor, execution for stealing a loaf or a few trinkets, public hangings, transportation. Morbid interest in murderers and their executions has been exploited in the popular press. So A. E. Housman was expressing a popular mood:

On moonlit heath and lonesome bank
The sheep beside me graze;
And yon the gallows used to clank
Fast by the four cross ways.

A careless shepherd once would keep
The flocks by moonlight there,
And high amongst the glimmering sheep
The dead man stood on air.

They hang us now in Shrewsbury Jail:
The whistles blow forlorn,
And trains all night groan on the rail
To men that die at dawn.

There sleeps in Shrewsbury Jail to-night,
Or wakes, as may betide,
A better lad, if things were right,
Than most that sleep outside.

The Ballad of Reading Gaol by Oscar Wilde derives from this poem. Then, of course, there is always the virile swagger—

Ale, man, ale's the stuff to drink
For fellows whom it hurts to think:
Look into the pewter pot
To see the world as the world's not.

In these poems there is, for all their apparent simplicity, a subtle art. We have it in that famous lyric, 'Bredon Hill', where Housman adds a fifth line to the ordinary common English measure of the four line stanza, and each time it has a different effect. In the first stanza it prolongs the clang of the bells—

In summertime on Bredon
The bells they sound so clear;
Round both the shires they ring them
In steeples far and near,
A happy noise to hear.

When the sweetheart dies and her coffn is carried into the

church, the extra line, isolated, apart, gives us all that tragedy of death.

> But when the snows at Christmas
> On Bredon top were strown,
> My love rose up so early
> And stole out unbeknown
> And went to church alone.

We may suspect that part of the popular appeal of *The Shropshire Lad* was due to its fatalism, as in the case of Fitzgerald's *Ruba'iyyat*. Fatalism, stoical endurance, is more than a philosophy; it is, perhaps, one of the primary instincts of the human race in its strange history on this earth through ages of earthquake, flood, fire, war.

The young poets of the thirties, in their revolt against the previous generation, concentrated most of their attack on *The Shropshire Lad*. I do not think this attack was due to its immense popularity. They may have detected in a number of poems an underlying sentimentality.

Oscar Wilde is best known as a wit, writer of brilliant social comedies, essayist and critic. His poetry has been dismissed in literary histories although it was widely liked. Only 'The Ballad of Reading Gaol' has escaped censure. Certainly his verse is full of echoes: Keats, Matthew Arnold, Swinburne, Baudelaire. Nevertheless his early Greek narratives are pleasant and some of his short poems are distinctive. His novel, *The Picture of Dorian Gray*, published in 1892, was much influenced by *A Rebours*, an imaginative study in decadence, by the Belgian writer, Huysmans. In the strict sense Wilde's novel is not really decadent. No doubt there are hints in it of mysterious evil and horrible vices, but the exigencies of the allegorical plot necessitated a moral in which he could scarcely have believed. Dorian Gray, the handsome young protagonist, remains young despite the years and his dissipated life. The strange protrait painted of him is hidden away and at times Dorian Gray looks at it and sees on it the increasing signs of his ill life. Still young and beautiful in his old age, he ventures to examine the portrait once more and is so shocked by the horrible face depicted on the canvas that he dies. He is found, an ugly old man, lying on the floor while above on the wall is the portrait of the beautiful young man whom all had known for so many years. Did Wilde take a hint for his plot from Hawthorne's allegorical story, *The Prophetic Pictures*? *Salome*, a one-act tragedy, written in French and published in 1893, was inspired by the sadistic painting by Gustave Moreau of the step-daughter of Herod gazing at the severed head of John the Baptist. In its brief doom-laden sentences and repeated phrases, it borrows the new dramatic technique of Maeterlinck, who had become fashionable. It is a complete expression of the *Fin de Siècle*.

Quite unexpectedly, Wilde turned to the brilliant tradition of social comedy, and we may suspect that he looked to the theatre because it afforded a wider public for the carefully prepared epigrams with which he amused the guests at the dining tables of the wealthy in London. So he revived with superb skill the method of eighteenth century comedies, most of which were written by Anglo-Irish writers: George Farquhar and William Congreve—really belonging to the Restoration period—Oliver Goldsmith, Richard Brinsley Sheridan, and lesser known dramatists such as Arthur Murphy and John O'Keeffe. It is generally agreed that the gift of these Anglo-Irish dramatists was helped by the fact that they had no loyalty to either country and so could observe with amusement the London social scene. In a little-known essay, Sir John Squire pointed out for the first time that Oscar Wilde had derived his paradoxical wit from the brilliant and half-forgotten novels of Disraeli, which he found on his mother's bookshelves in Merrion Square, Dublin, in his early years. Disraeli's method was to reverse a well-known axiom. To give an example, 'He was born of poor but dishonest parents'. It seems a simple trick but the problem is first to catch your proverb. In this age of specialization, it is a wise thing to remember that the that the early work of poet, dramatist or novelist usually shows the formative influence of one or other of the forgotten authors who were popular during his youth.

The spectacular downfall of Oscar Wilde, his trial and imprisonment, his miserable death in 1900, ended an epoch. With righteous self-satisfaction, the public might well declare: "That is the end of Art for Art's Sake!"

The Celtic Twilight

The Celtic Twilight School, of which W. B. Yeats was the acknowledged leader, became fashionable during the nineties and had considerable influence: its delicate impressionism, its shadowy themes, other-worldly longings and subtle wavering rhythms were in accord with the *Fin de Siècle* Movement. At the close of the century, the inevitable reaction came and it was an extreme one. Even Yeats had to reject eventually its mode and turned in dislike from his early poetry. It is interesting to note that no study of the Celtic Twilight as a whole has yet been published. We have had an increasing number of books about Yeats, but in all of them his early work is described as pre-Raphaelite and there are the inevitable references to a vague Celticism. This attitude is partly due to the aversion with which these critics have regarded all the work which Yeats wrote before the age of fifty, and partly to the fact that they have studied him more or less as an isolated figure and have neglected to study his background or period sufficiently. Their view that Celtic mythology, unlike that of other countries, is dim and vague, could have been quickly corrected if they had turned to any translation of our sagas. Had they considered that Yeats spent a number of years experimenting in this new Twilight mode and developing its subtle art, they would scarcely have described its impressionistic methods as vague.

Yeats has explained in one of his critical essays that it took him a long time to expel the Italian light of Shelley from his poems. When he began to write, the great influence was still that of Tennyson, which had spread to Ireland in the middle of the Victorian age. You will find it in Aubrey de Vere, William Allingham, T. C. Irwin and other writers. How far it had gone will be seen from an anthology of Nineteenth Century Irish Poets compiled by the late Geoffrey Taylor. Yeats never

31

referred to Tennyson in any of his critical essays but I think we can speak of a secret, indirect influence. In 'The Voyage of Maeldune,' Tennyson had taken one of the Gaelic legends of voyages to the earthly paradise. We may assume that his example inspired the young poet when he set out to write a similar legend in *The Wanderings of Oisin*. In English literary tradition, fairies and elemental spirits had been regarded lightly as 'the wee folk' and as sprites. Even Shakespeare, in his comedy, *A Midsummer Night's Dream*, did not take them too seriously. Tennyson was the first to write of them imaginatively in *The Idylls of the King*. Here is a passage from 'Guinevere', which anticipates, I think, the quality and mood of the Celtic Twilight. The situation is a dramatic one. A little novice is talking to Guinevere, who has retired to a convent. Little does the young girl realise that she is talking to the Queen herself. Here is part of what she says:—

The land was full of signs
And wonders ere the coming of the Queen.
So said my father, and himself was knight
Of the great Table—at the founding of it;
And rode thereto from Lyonesse, and he said:
That as he rode, an hour or maybe twain
After the sunset, down the coast, he heard
Strange music, and he paused, and turning—there,
All down the lonely coast of Lyonesse,
Each with a beacon-star upon his head,
And with a wild sea-light about his feet,
He saw them—headland after headland flame
Far on into the rich heart of the west:
And in the light the white mermaiden swam,
And strong man-breasted things stood from the sea,
And sent a deep sea-voice thro' all the land,
To which the little elves of chasm and cleft
Made answer, sounding like a distant horn.
So said my father—yea, and furthermore,

32

Next morning, while he passed the dim-lit woods,
Himself beheld three spirits mad with joy
Come dashing down on a tall wayside flower,
That shook beneath them, as the thistle shakes
When three grey linnets wrangle for the seed:
And still at evening on before his horse
The flickering fairy-cycle wheel'd and broke
Flying, for all the land was full of life.
And when at last he came to Camelot,
A wreath of airy dancers hand-in-hand
Swung round the lighted lantern on the hall;
And in the hall itself was such a feast
As never man had dream'd; for every knight
Had whatsoever meat he long'd for served
By hands unseen; and even as he said
Down in the cellars merry bloated things
Shoulder'd the spigot, straddling on the butts
While the wine ran: so glad were spirits and men
Before the coming of the sinful Queen.

The description there of the fairy circle of dance is surely
not very different in mood from Yeats's poem, 'The Host-
ing of the Sidhe'. There is another influence from Tennyson
which has not been noticed. Yeats may not have shared
the strict Victorian morality of the Poet Laureate, but his
early poetry has the same refinement and purity, the same
ideal of romantic love. Those early books of his, with their
dark blue richly gilt covers, could be left safely on the table
in any drawing-room; they could not bring a blush to any
cheek.

There is, I suggest, another secret influence, one which
I did not suspect for a long time. Owing to his interest in
theosophy and Buddhism, Yeats had written several poems
on Indian subjects, such as the small dramatic scene,
'Anashuya and Vijaya' and 'The Indian to his Love', and
I often wondered at their exactness. Then I suddenly
remembered that Sir Edwin Arnold was a well-known poet
of the time and his long poem, 'The Light of Asia', became

a best-seller. In it and in another long poem, he expounded the sacred Books of the East. His lines are filled with exotic detail for he knew India well and had been a schoolteacher there.

In his first poems on Irish subjects, Yeats had endeavoured to write literary ballads, which would have the direct simple appeal of the traditional ballad, in itself a difficult task. To find the right way of expressing the Twilight mood and evoking the traditional fairy world was a more difficult and sophisticated task. With remarkable perception, he had noticed the delayed rhythm which Thomas Moore had discovered in Irish folk music and used in two of the lyrics in his collection of Irish Melodies. The best-known of these two begins—

> At the mid hour of night, when stars are weeping, I fly
> To the lone vale we loved, when life shone warm in thine eye,
> And I think oft, if spirits can steal from the regions of air
> To revisit past scenes of delight, thou wilt come to me there,
> And tell me our love is remember'd even in the sky.

Yeats used this rhythm in a poem which was to pursue him, with its popularity for many years, 'The Lake Isle of Inisfree'. Samuel Ferguson also had borrowed this slow, slightly irregular rhythm in several of his translations of Irish traditional poems. Callanan's translation, 'The Outlaw of Loch Lene' is another fine example of this measure. Although I had known that lyrical Ulster ballad, 'The Fairy Thorn', by Ferguson, I did not realise until A. E. told me so that it anticipated all the elements of the Celtic Twilight. Here are the dim hues and the long Irish twilight, the mystery and suggestion, the delayed rhythm and a vowel-music suggested by Gaelic internal assonance. The poem tells how three girls, who dance at dusk around the forbidden tree, are drawn within the ring of enchantment.

34

They're glancing through the glimmer of the quiet eve,
Away in milky wavings of neck and ankle bare;
The heavy-sliding stream in its sleepy song they leave,
And the crags in the ghostly air.

The dance ends in a dread hush:

Thus clasped and prostrate all, with their heads
together bowed,
Soft o'er their bosoms beating—the only human
sound—
They hear the silky footsteps of the silent fairy crowd,
Like a river in the air gliding round.

When I first discovered for myself the poetry of the
Celtic Twilight period, as a young student, I found it almost impossible to understand. I groped through a mist of
my own over lines which I could not scan according to
the rules. It was quite unlike English poetry which we
learned in our class or the Gaelic poetry which we studied
in another class. I had never heard of symbolism or impressionism. However, when I had made the Grand Tour
of English literature, the difficulties were gone. It was
pleasant to escape for a while from the law and order of
English poetry into that shadowy world of subdued speech
and nuance.

In the first lyrics of Yeats about the Unseen World,
come of them never reprinted, the fairies or elves were
fanciful, like those of Allingham; then, as the theme became
more subtle, the poet endeavoured to suggest the fairy
music, the enchantment, the allurement. From this came his
slow experiments in finding delicate cadences and evasive
rhythms. In 1893, Yeats published a prose collection of
sketches and tales of Sligo, entitled *The Celtic Twilight*.
There is a piece in it called 'The Visionary', which gives
us a glimpse of his friend, A.E. and his own mystical
interests.

A young man came to see me at my lodgings the other
night, and began to talk of the making of the earth and
the heavens and much else. I questioned him about his

35

life and doings. He had written many poems and painted many mystical designs since we last met, but latterly had neither written nor painted, for his whole heart was set upon making his mind strong, vigorous and calm, and the emotional life of the artist was bad for him, he feared. He recited his poems readily. Some, indeed, had never been written down. These, with their wild music as of winds blowing in the reeds, seemed to me the very inmost voice of Celtic sadness, and of Celtic longing for infinite things the world has never seen. The poetry he recited to me was full of his nature and his visions. Sometimes it told of other lives he believes himself to have lived in other centuries, sometimes of people he had talked to, revealing them to their own minds. I told him I would write an article upon him and it and was told in turn that I might do so if I did not mention his name, for he wished always to be 'unknown, obscure, impersonal'.

To A.E., nature spirits were part of a mystical universe of polytheism. Yeats, who was not as untroubled a believer as his friend, found himself committed to his fairies. He had to defend himself against the charge of superstition. However, spiritualism was fashionable in many London circles and theosophy had brought back an interest not only in eastern religions but in mediaeval magic, alchemy and rosicrucianism. In the lyric, 'To Ireland in the Coming Times', Yeats, by way of poetic apology, boldly declared his aims, his literary ambition, his adherence to the contemporary aesthetic cult of beauty symbolised by the rose, his practice of magic, and Ireland is presented as still in the twilight of the ages:

Nor may I less be counted one
With Davis, Mangan, Ferguson,
Because to him who ponders well,
My rhymes more than their rhyming tell
Of the dim wisdom old and deep,
That God gives unto man in sleep.

36

For the elemental beings go
About my table to and fro.
In flood and fire and clay and wind,
They huddle from man's pondering mind;
Yet he who treads in austere ways
May surely meet their ancient gaze.
Man ever journeys on with them
After the red-rose-bordered hem.
Ah, faeries, dancing under the moon,
A Druid land, a Druid tune!

Well, that picture of a young poet at his writing-desk, surrounded by obedient spirits, a young Faust, who had not to sell his soul, still makes large demands on our belief. To maintain such an attitude, day in, night out, must have required considerable courage in a poet who suffered from shyness and we must applaud the courage shown. In the later version, which is contradictory in mood, Yeats wrote:

For the elemental creatures go
About my table to and fro,
That hurry from unmeasured mind
To rant and rage in flood and wind.

What would the spirits have thought of this revision!

Those early books of Yeats, however shadowy and dim they were in substance, were brought out in dark blue covers gleaming with gold leaf, and the mood of the lyrics harmonised with that of the *Fin de Siècle*. Yeats scarcely knew any French, but Arthur Symons was there to tell him of the occult drama, *Axel's Castle,* by Villiers de l'Isle Adam, with its mediaeval symbolism; and already the plays of Maeterlinck, with their modern use of the symbolist method, were coming into fashion. Ireland had become mistier, more druidical and, like the Lady of Shallott, he saw it at a second remove. As he wrote to a friend: 'The old tales were still alive for me, indeed, but with a new, strange, half-unreal life, as if in a wizard glass'.

The Wind among the Reeds, a small collection of choice

lyrics, took more than seven years in the writing and did not appear until 1897. Here the twilight mood is elaborated with careful art. Many of these lyrics, so evocative, so individual in their music, very often are only a few lines in length:

O, curlew, cry no more on the air,
Or only to the water in the West;
Because your crying brings to my mind
Passion-dimmed eyes and long heavy hair
That was shaken out over my breast:
There is enough evil in the crying of the wind.

In this evocative manner, Yeats can probably go no further than such lines as these:

You need but lift a pearl-pale hand,
And bind up your long hair and sigh;
And all men's hearts must burn and beat;
And candle-like foam on the dim sand,
And stars climbing the dew-dropping sky,
Live but to light your passing feet.

These poems of reverential, unhappy love echo the mood of the *Vita Nuova* of Dante, as indicated by the very titles: 'He remembers forgotten Beauty', 'He bids his Beloved be at Peace', 'To his Heart, bidding it have no Fear'. Symbolism is now used deliberately and some of the symbols are drawn from Celtic mythology. Nowadays these poems may seem perhaps to belong to a rather deliberate self-conscious mode. Although Yeats came to reject the Celtic Twilight, I do not think he ever escaped from it. The legendary music of the Sidhe is still in the background. As late as 1917, Yeats was still enthralled by it, although his poetry had become austere.

At the grey round of the hill
Music of a lost kingdom
Runs, runs and is suddenly still.
The winds out of Clare-Galway
Carry it: suddenly it is still.

38

I have heard in the night air
A wandering airy music;
And moidered in that snare
A man is lost of a sudden,
In that sweet wandering snare.

Other examples might be quoted. For instance, in *The Tower*, written in 1928, the section with the elaborate sub-title, 'I see Phantoms of Hatred and of the Heart's Fullness and of the Coming Emptiness', shows the twilight mood still expressed and contrasted with the new age of violence. Surely also there is significance in the fact that the last two legendary poems written by the poet in 1939, a few weeks before his death, 'Cuchulain Comforted' and 'The Black Tower', though stark in manner and obscure in their symbolism, are a return to the Celtic Twilight.

Modestly and under the pseudonym of A.E., George Russell published his first book, *Homeward, Songs by the Way*, in 1894, unobtrusively. Despite this, it attracted quite a lot of attention. It is remarkably mature and complete; one would never suspect that it was written by a young man in his twenties. The poems are mystical and some of them are rather obscure. In these meditative remote poems, we have the same twilight which we find in those of Yeats, but here the twilight changes into the jewelled reflection of night.

Its edges foamed with amethyst and rose,
Withers once more the old blue flower of day:
There where the ether like a diamond glows
Its petals fade away.

A shadowy tumult stirs the dusky air;
Sparkle the delicate dews, the distant snows;
The great deep thrills, for through it everywhere
The breath of Beauty blows.

I saw how all the trembling ages past,
Moulded to her by deep and deeper breath,
Neared to the hour when Beauty breathes her last
And knows herself in death.

And here is the first stanza of another poem as an example of the poetic convention which the young poet had discovered for himself and used in his visional lines—

When the breath of twilight blows to flame the misty skies,
All its vaporous sapphire, violent glow and silver gleam
With their magic flood me through the gateway of the eyes;
I am one with the twilight's dream.

The title of the poem, 'By the Margin of the Great Deep', gives us a clue to its inner significance: that dream is taking place on the verge of infinity. The metre of A.E.'s poems remains simple and unvaried, but at times the lyrics have a light subtle movement:—

Those delicate wanderers—
The wind, the star, the cloud—
Ever before mine eyes,
As to an altar bowed,
Light and dew-laden airs
Offer in sacrifice.

The offerings arise:
Hazes of rainbow light,
Pure crystal, blue, and gold,
Through dreamland take their flight;
And 'mid the sacrifice
God moveth as of old.

In miracles of fire
He symbols forth His days;
In gleams of crystal light
Reveals what pure pathways
Lead to the soul's desire,
The silence of the height.

You will note the use of the word, symbol. Yeats never used this word in his poems, but it is used a number of times by A.E. and, in fact, one of his poems is entitled 'Symbolism'. Here is the first verse:

40

Now when the giant in us wakes and broods,
Filled with home-yearnings, drowsily he flings
From his deep heart high dreams and mystic moods,
Mixed with the memory of the loved earth-things;
Clothing the vast with a familiar face,
Reaching his right hand forth to greet the starry race.

But there are different kinds of symbols and some are deceptive, and this is the theme of a poem entitled 'The Symbol Seduces'. In 'Star Teachers', we have the true way of symbols:

For this, for this the lights innumerable
As symbols shine that we the true light win:
For every star and every deep they fill
Are stars and deeps within.

As you know, all mystics claim that their spiritual experiences are inexpressible: the higher states of the mind are beyond mere words. So the poet mystic can only suggest them by hint and symbol. Outwardly many of the lines of A.E. may seem simple, as when he writes:—

In the fire of love we live, or pass by many ways,
By unnumbered ways of dream to death.

Here there are subtle implications and if they evade us, we are left with a generalised feeling.

At this time Yeats and A.E. would have been unaware of the Symbolist movement in Europe and their use of symbols was due to their interest in theosophy and the Sacred Books of the East. I think, however, that A.E.'s use of the imagery of precious jewels and metals was inspired by the Book of Revelations. Rémy de Gourmont, in *La Latin Mystique*, describes a school of apocalytic poets in the early Christian centuries, who drew similar imagery from that book. A.E.'s delight in colour was due, no doubt, to the fact that he was not only a poet, but also a painter. Occasionally he drew on Gaelic mythology and his poem, 'Dana', for instance, shows how closely he and Yeats shared the twilight mood. It begins—

I am the tender voice calling 'Away',

Whispering between the beatings of the heart . . .
and it goes on—

> And I weave
> My spells at evening, folding with dim caress,
> Aerial arms, and twilight-dropping hair,
> The lonely wanderer by shore or wood . . .

And here is the concluding passage: —

> I breathe
> A deeper pity than all love, myself
> Mother of all, but without hands to heal,
> Too vast and vague—they know me not! But yet
> I am the heartbreak over fallen things,
> The sudden gentleness that stays the blow;
> And I am in the kiss that warriors give
> Pausing in battle, and in the tears that fall
> Over the vanquished foe; and in the highest
> Among the Danaan gods I am the last
> Council of mercy in their hearts, where they
> Mete justice from a thousand starry thrones.

In this lyric there is a suggestion of a famous poem by
Emerson, 'Brahma', but this is one of the very few influences which we find in the early work of A.E. Emerson's
mystical philosophy, however, had a powerful influence
both on A.E. and Yeats. His Oversoul is the *Anima Mundi*
of Yeats.

In London, Lionel Johnson, as I have noted in my talk
on the *Fin de Siècle,* was one of the first to be influenced
by the Celtic Twilight mood. He was of Irish descent and
his poem, 'Ways of War', was much admired by Thomas
MacDonagh. It begins: —

> A terrible and splendid trust
> Heartens the host of Innisfail:
> Their dream is of the swift sword-thrust,
> A lightning glory of the Gael.

Johnson had also a Welsh strain and set a few vague twilight lyrics against the Welsh background, as in his poem,
'To Morfydd'—

A voice on the winds,
A voice by the waters,
Wanders and cries:
Oh! what are the winds,
And what are the waters,
Mine are your eyes!

The poem dissolves in musicality.

Surprisingly enough, even Arthur Symons was lured by all this faery music. 'In the Wood of Finvara' begins well—

I have grown tired of sorrow and human tears;
Life is a dream in the night, a fear among fears,
A naked runner lost in a storm of spears.

But it ends with almost a parody of Yeats—

Here, in the fairy wood, between sea and sea,
I have heard the song of a fairy bird in a tree,
And the peace that is not in the world has flown to me.

'The Crying of Water' is almost worse—

O water, voice of my heart, crying in the sand,
All night long crying with a mournful cry,
As I lie and listen, and cannot understand
The voice of my heart in my side or the voice of the sea.

An English convert to the School was Nora Hopper, and Yeats wrote delightedly of her:

'Even now, when the first enchantment is gone and I see faults I was blind to, I cannot go by certain brown bogs covered with white tufts of bog-cotton—places where the world seems to become faint and fragile—without remembering the verses her Daluan—a kind of Irish Pan—sings among the bogs; and when once I remember them, they run in my head for hours—

All the way to Tir na n'Og are many roads that run,
But the darkest road is trodden by the King of Ireland's son.
The world wears on to sundown, and love is lost and won.

But he recks not of loss or gain, the King of Ireland's son.
He follows on for ever, when all your chase is done,
He follows after shadows—the King of Ireland's son.
One does not know why he sings it ,or why he dies on November Eve, or why the men cry over him "Daluan is dead—dead! Daluan is dead!" and the women, "Da Mort is king," for "Daluan" is but Monday and "Da Mort" is but Tuesday'.

Then appeared the mysterious Fiona Macleod, who introduced the Celtic Twilight into Scotland. Yeats and A.E. corresponded with this mysterious lady of the north. But eventually it turned out that these twilight poems and stories of the Hebrides were really written by a well-known critic and literary man, William Sharp. Was it a case of dual personality or had he collaborated with a mysterious Fiona Macleod? That was one of the minor problems of the time. 'The Immortal Hour', a lyrical drama, by Fiona Macleod, was later turned into an opera by the English composer, Rutland Boughton, and proved successful.

Among the younger Irish followers of the School were three women poets, Eva Gore Booth, Ella Young and Susan Mitchell, who also wrote witty humorous poems and parodies. These three writers were also theosophists and were more influenced by A.E. than by Yeats. James Cousins, a narrative poet, shared the new belief; and, in passing, I should like to mention also a fine ballad, 'The Love Talker', by Eithne Carbery.

Seamus O'Sullivan, in his early poems, achieved a delicacy in the use of subtle wavering rhythms comparable with that of Yeats, and he widened the range of the mood. In his lyric, 'The Twilight People', he hints at the long centuries of oppression, exile and despair: —

It is a whisper among the hazel bushes;
It is a long low whispering voice that fills
With a sad music the bending and swaying rushes;
It is a heart-beat deep in the quiet hills.

Twilight people, why will you still be crying,
Crying and calling to me out of the trees?
For under the quiet grass the wise are lying,
And all the strong ones are gone over the seas.

And I am old, and in my heart at your calling,
Only the old dead dreams a-fluttering go;
As the wind, the forest wind, in its falling
Sets the withered leaves fluttering to and fro.

Later Seumas O'Sullivan moved on to what we might call a Georgian twilight of his own, in which he evokes the quiet side-streets of Dublin at twilight, the Georgian houses, the tenements, which were once aristocratic dwellings—in fact, that Dublin which we are now destroying so rapidly.

Lastly, if one has to defend this movement of the nineties, which is now out of fashion, one may say that it was realistic in its acceptance of our lowering skies. Much of English poetry exists in an ideal sunshine, that of Greece and Rome. We have almost to go back to Anglo-Saxon alliterative staves to find the mists and twilight of the northern latitude. And how exact some of the images and descriptions are! Yeats, in his masterly way, could express in a single line the atmosphere of Connemara, 'the wet winds are blowing out of the clinging air.'

In 1920, when the vogue of the movement had long since passed, the well-known Scottish dramatist, J. M. Barrie, published a play called *Mary Rose*, which was very successful, though the shorter *Cambridge History of Literature* has dismissed it as 'a disconcerting ghost story, which conveyed the impression that the author had got lost in a Tir na nOg of his own and could not find his way back'. This seems to me too harsh and, seen against the background of the Twilight School, I think the play has some interest. A young honeymoon couple in the west of Scotland go out on an excursion to an uninhabited isle, regarded locally with superstition. The young bride, Mary Rose, runs happily towards a hollow and when her husband reaches it, he finds that she has vanished. Fifteen or twenty years elapse and then suddenly Mary Rose is found on the island. She is still the young bride, untouched by time, and believes that she has been only a few seconds away. The last act is tragic, very moving. Her aged parents and her middle-aged husband are waiting to meet her. In this symbolic play, Barrie confronts superstition and reality. The reality may be regarded as a final comment on the Celtic Twilight—but not quite. The last word was with James Joyce.

In his first phase, Joyce was fascinated by the Celtic Twilight mood and this is obvious as we read *The Portrait of the Artist*. In *Chamber Music,* most of the poems are delicate experiments in Elizabethan lyric form, but a few echo the Celtic Twilight mood. The best of them is inspired by 'The Unappeasable Host', which appeared in *The Wind among the Reeds*. Joyce's poem begins—

> I hear an army charging upon the land,
> And the thunder of horses plunging, foam about their knees:
> Arrogant, in black armour, behind them stand,
> Disdaining the reins, with fluttering whips, the charioteers.

'Black armour' is a striking phrase but, alas, it was first used by Lionel Johnson in one of his sonnets. Joyce would have read the poem in *A Treasury of Irish Poetry,* edited by Stopford Brooke and T. W. Rolleston, published in 1900. Years later Joyce was still lured by the Twilight mood, as in the song 'She weeps over Rahoon', which appeared in *Pomes Penyeach.*

> Rain on Rahoon falls softly, softly falling,
> Where my dark lover lies.
> Sad is his voice that calls me, sadly calling,
> At grey moonrise.
>
> Love, hear thou
> How soft, how sad his voice is ever calling,

Ever unanswered, and the dark rain falling,
Then as now.

Some have admired this melancholy lyric. It seems to be like the poem of Arthur Symons which I have quoted, a parody.

But Joyce was not yet done with the Celtic Twilight. The best-known passage of *Finnegans Wake*, which Joyce chose when he was making a recording, sums up, I think, the Celtic Twilight. In the passage, Anna Livia Plurabelle is described as 'just a young thin pale shy slim slip of a thing then, sauntering by Silvamoon lake'. The twilight deepens and the shadowy figures of the mythic washerwomen can no longer be seen; the only sounds are those of flowing water and of the coming night.

Can't hear with the waters of. The chittering waters of. Flittering bats, fieldmice bawk talk. Ho! Are you not gone ahome? What Thom Malone? Can't hear with the bawk of bats, all thim liffeying waters of. Ho, talk save us! My foos wont moos. I feel as old as yonder elm. A tale told of Shaun or Shem? All Livia's daughter-sons. Dark hawks hear us. Night! Night! My ho head halls. I feel as heavy as yonder stone. Tell me of John or Shaun? Who were Shem and Shaun the living sons and daughters of? Night now! Tell me, tell me, tell me, elm. Night night! Telmetale of stem or stone. Beside the rivering waters of, hither and thithering waters of. Night!

Whatever its literary value, I think the Celtic Twilight phase, like Macpherson's *Ossian*, long out of fashion, is well worth research. The Revival, as we call it, began when Yeats and others turned away from Irish rhetorical, political poetry and the Parnell controversy. I have tried to suggest how the Celtic Twilight phase spread, and how it was influenced by the *Fin de Siècle* mood abroad, and, in turn, how it exercised some influence elsewhere. To some of these writers it was more than a literary phase: it involved visionary experience. Wordsworth, though not a mystic, had a mystical view of nature. These writers had a similar

47

view of ancient Ireland; and this is an aspect that has been overlooked.

As late as 1898, in a short essay entitled 'The Autumn of the Body', Yeats wrote: 'I see, indeed, in the arts of every country those faint energies which many call "the decadence," and which I, because I believe that the arts lie dreaming of things to come, prefer to call the autumn of the body. An Irish poet whose rhythms are like the cry of a sea-bird in autumn twilight has told its meaning in the line, "The very sunlight's weary, and it's time to quit the plough." Its importance is the greater because it comes to us at the moment when we are beginning to be interested in many things which positive science, the interpreter of exterior law, has always denied: communion of mind with mind in thought and without words, foreknowledge in dreams and in visions, and the coming among us of the dead, and of much else. We are, it may be, at a crowning crisis of the world, at the moment when man is about to ascend, with the wealth he has been so long gathering upon his shoulders, the stairway he has been descending from the first days.' And he adds: 'Man has wooed and won the world, and has fallen weary, and not, I think, for a time, but with a weariness that will not end until the last autumn, when the stars shall be blown away like withered leaves.' Here is what James Cousins, who settled down in India and became a well-known Professor of English, wrote in the Preface to his *Collected Poems,* published in New York in 1932:

The Irish Literary Revival circumferenced my poetical life. Thereafter, that vision and enthusiasm became its centre—and circumferences learned not to matter...
The personalities and events of the Irish Mythos, which was the deepest inspiration of the movement, had become to me the imaginative incarnation of powers and processes in the universe and in myself. I felt that its vision was more ultimate than insight and more prophetic than foresight; and through its contemplation and embodi-

48

ment in my early poems I aspired towards the capacity to
see the significance of the insignificant and to feel the
eternal in the temporal.

With the turn of the century, the younger poets, Padraic
Colum, Joseph Campbell and others had turned to more
mundane matters in their poems of country life; and later
Synge, in his reaction against the Twilight, declared:

'It may almost be said that before verse can be human
again it must learn to be brutal'.

Let me end with his well-known poem, directed as much
against Yeats as against A.E. It is entitled 'The Passing of
the Shee: After looking at one of A.E.'s pictures'—

Adieu, sweet Angus, Maeve, and Fand,
Ye plumed yet skinny Shee,
That poets played with hand in hand
To learn their ecstasy.

We'll stretch in Red Dan Sally's ditch,
And drink in Tubber fair,
Or poach with Red Dan Philly's bitch
The badger and the hare.

Victorian Verse Drama

The course of poetic drama in the last century was remarkable and foreigners might well consider it eccentric and therefore very British. Interest in the form was revived during the Romantic Movement and spread in the Victorian age. Famous poets, such as Wordsworth, Coleridge, Walter Savage Landor, Byron, Shelley, Tennyson, Browning, Swinburne, wrote five-act tragedies in blank verse, each hoping to recapture the glories of the Elizabethan period. Soon it became a fashion to write in a pseudo-Shakespearean style. Unlike Shakespeare and the other Elizabethan dramatists, however, none of these Victorian writers had any practical knowledge of the stage and most of their plays were unactable. So we get a new form known as closet drama, or plays for the study, like the second part of Goethe's *Faust*. In these plays, the acts and the speeches of the characters in them gradually become larger and out of all proportion. In Swinburne's immense trilogy about Mary, Queen of Scots, the second act of 'Bothwell' has twenty-one scenes. The limit was reached in Thomas Hardy's epic drama about the Napoleonic wars, *The Dynasts,* which was not published until 1904. The play has 125 scenes.

A few lesser poets had a practical knowledge of dramatic technique, and one of the last of these was Stephen Phillips whose first play, *Paolo and Francesca,* was published in 1899. He had been a member of Sir Frank Benson's company. His ensuing plays, such as *Herod, Ulysses, Nero,* were lavishly praised by critics, for here at last it seemed that the great secret dream of reviving the drama of the past had been realised. But there was a swift reaction. The plays of Phillips are now regarded unfairly as merely theatrical in effect and Tennysonian in style. Later Laurence Binyon, Gordon Bottomley, T. S. Eliot, W. H. Auden and others were less ambitious. Professor Allardyce Nicholls wrote a study of early nineteenth century drama but, to the best of my knowledge, no complete history of English verse drama from its beginnings has yet been written.

So the Victorian age had its great poets, novelists, critics, historians, but no verse drama of consequence, no prose plays of literary interest. Serious drama was not resumed until 1892 when an Irish writer, described amusingly by W. B. Yeats as a man with a mind like a sewing machine, had his first play produced at the small Court Theatre in London. It was called *Widowers' Houses* and the writer's name was George Bernard Shaw; the play was howled down by the audience and denounced by the critics. What was the reason of this lack of drama in the great Victorian age? Academic critics have tried to hush up the subject or offer excuses: the theatre had become commercialized; there was a state censorship on religion, morality, politics. Even novelists, such as Dickens, George Eliot, Thackeray, owing to public opinion, had to keep to the fairy tale of the kindly stork and the gooseberry bush. I believe that an English dramatist with the genius of Ibsen would have faced all difficulties. As it was, melodrama, entertainments, comedies adapted from Scribe and other commercial French playwrights, held the stage.

Curiously enough, the long tradition of verse drama lingered on the stage and was helped by the fact that Shakespeare had become popular and was still played. The actor-managers wanted other heroic tragedies in which they and their actors could rave and rant. The verse might be very bad but they could put passion into the lines and, if necessary, tear it to bits.

During the Restoration period, prose comedies prevailed. Its chief dramatists were Anglo-Irish: Farquhar, Congreve, with two fine English dramatists, Wycherley and Etheridge. Later in the century came Goldsmith, Richard Brinsley Sheridan and lesser-known dramatists, like John O'Keeffe and Arthur Murphy. The best-known verse play of the time of Charles II. was *Venice Preserved* by Thomas Otway, which was popular for long on the stage though it now seems tedious and over-strained. A thin tradition of neo-classic plays persisted—from Addison's *Cato* to Johnson's chilly *Irene*—despite the mockery of the new prose writers. The Duke of Buckingham had satirised Dryden's heroic drama in *The Rehearsal;* Fielding parodied classic tragedies in *Tom Thumb,* and Henry Cary, best known for a delightful song, 'Sally in our Alley', made fun of them all in a short skit, *Chrononhotonthologos.* With the coming of the gothic novels by Mrs. Radcliffe, Horace Walpole and Monk Lewis, and the first stirrings of the Romantic Movement, there was an increase of historical and horrific blank-verse tragedies. Irish writers, unfortunately, shared in the vogue. In the Georgian era, Sir Aubrey de Vere, a friend of Wordsworth, wrote a poetic tragedy about Mary Tudor; Charles Maturin indited a horror drama in verse; later John Banim wrote a classical verse drama which was produced at Covent Garden in 1840. Everyone was scribbling verse dramas and, as far as I know, there has been no comprehensive history of them. Many of them were bad; the best of them poetically were unactable.

Schiller was the great pioneer of verse drama in Germany and he was a practical dramatist for he began by producing plays. His highly successful romantic play, *The Robbers,* influenced the young Wordsworth and Coleridge. In his preface to *The Borderers,* written long afterwards, Wordsworth tell us that he did not intend the play for the stage. Schiller's play is violent in action; Wordsworth's is mild and prosaic in its verse. Coleridge's play, *Remorse,* was stronger and had a brief success on the stage.

Byron wrote a number of tragedies but disdained the stage itself. Among these plays are *Marino Faliero, Manfred, Cain.* His plays are romantic in mood although he was influenced to some degree by Racine and later by Alfieri. One play, however, *Sardanapalus,* observes strictly the three classical unities. I heard, by chance, some years ago on the B.B.C. a production of his somewhat Miltonic play, *Cain*, a play which has usually been dismissed by the literary critics. It is, of course, a typical expression of Byronic gloom, but it seems to me effective.

Shelley also wanted to write a play for the London stage but, unfortunately, in *The Cenci*, he chose the forbidden theme of incest. In his preface, referring indirectly to Wordsworth's view of natural speech, he wrote:

'I entirely agree with those modern critics who assert that in order to move men to true sympathy we must use the familiar language of men, and that our great ancestors the ancient English poets are the writers, a study of whom might incite us to do that for our own age which they have done for theirs'.

In these lines Shelley anticipates the attitude of the critics of our own day. I do not think it can be held, however, that Shelley really achieved this in his play although he obviously tried to keep to plain language. He turned after that to lyrical drama, for the stage of the mind: *Hellas*, and the wonderful *Prometheus Unbound*.

Pseudo-Elizabethan drama off-stage really begins with Thomas Lovell Beddoes. His mother was a sister of Maria Edgeworth but there is no reference to this country in any of his writings. His lengthy plays, *Death's Jest-Book: or The Fool's Tragedy* (1825) and *The Brides' Tragedy* display his delight in the work of Webster and Cyril Tourneur. Dukes, unfortunate heroines, conspirators, assassins and bloody horrors fill these pages and the lines are full of violent or extraordinary images. Here is a mild example of his work:—

Isbrand:
> Come, let's be doing: we have talked whole nights
> Of what an instant, with one flash of action,
> Should have performed: you wise and speaking people
> Need some one, with a hatchet-stroke, to free
> The Pallas of your Jove-like headaches.

Duke:

> Patience:
> Fledging comes after hatching. One day more:
> This evening brings the wedding of our prince,
> And with it feasts and maskings. In mid bowls
> And giddy dances let us fall upon them.

Siegfried:

> Well thought: our enemies will be assembled.

Isbrand:

> I like to see Ruin at dinner time,
> Firing his cannons with the match they lit
> For the buck-roasting faggots. But what say you
> To what concerns you most? (*To Adalmar*)

Adalmar:

> That I am ready
> To hang my hopeful crown of happiness
> Upon the temple of the public good.

Beddoes is best known for his delicate lyrics, which might have been written in the Elizabethan age. Here is a stanza from one of them which suggests the lyrics of Webster:—

> The wind dead leaves and snow
> Doth hurry to and fro;
> And, once, a day shall break
> O'er the wave,
> When a storm of ghosts shall shake
> The dead, until they wake
> In the grave.

And here is a dirge which recalls John Ford:—

> If thou wilt ease thine heart
> Of love and all its smart,
> Then sleep, dear, sleep;
> And not a sorrow
> Hang any tear on your eyelashes;
> Lie still and deep,
> Sad soul, until the sea-wave washes
> The rim of the sun to-morrow
> In eastern sky.

54

George Darley, a neglected Irish poet, was a contemporary of Beddoes and, in fact, both died in the same year as Clarence Mangan, 1849. *Sylvia, or The May Queen* is one of the last of the pastoral dramas which began in the Elizabethan age. Darley, who lived near the Scalp, was, I think, inspired by the streams and woods of Co. Wicklow. Here is a pleasant passage from *Sylvia*: —

Sylvia:
Look at the feeding swan beneath the willows:
How pure her white neck gleams against their green
As she sits nesting on the waters!

Romanzo:
                             Beautiful!
She is the lady of the reed-girt Isles!
See! how she swells her navigable wings
And coasts her sedgy empire keenly round!
She looks a bird of snow dropt from the clouds
To queen it o'er the minnows!

Sylvia:
                           Doth she not,
Side-looking, slow, disdainful one!

Romanzo:
                           The bright,
The pearly creature!—Lone and calm she rides,
Like Dian on the wave when night is clear,
And the sleek west-wind smooths the billows-down
Into forgetfulness, that she may see
How fast her silver gondola can boom
Sheer on the level deep.

Sylvia:
                       Beyond yon rock
Down which a torrent shines afar; the noise
Is loud, yet we can't hear it.

Romanzo:
                       Partial Heaven!
O what a splendid deluge thou pour'st down
From out thy glorious flood-gate, on this vale!

Thickets, and knolls, slopes, lawns, and bosomy dells,
Scarce show their green for gold. Yet, it is strange!
There is a melancholy in sun-bright fields
Deeper to me than gloom; I am ne'er so sad
As when I sit amid bright scenes alone.

Darley settled down in London and his great ambition was
to write for the stage. He chose a fine historical theme,
which could not have been used by Shakespeare because
of religious reasons—the tragedy of Thomas-a-Becket. He
laboured over it for years and I suspect that this is why it
is so packed, so clogged with imagery. He must have been
tired as he got to the end of it, for the scene in the Cathedral when Becket is killed runs to only seventeen lines.
Here, as in Beddoes' plays, we have the same Elizabethan
violence of images. This is an example: a statesman,
rushing in from the royal council room, exclaims:

Pshaw! a delicate storm
To that within! Could'st stretch thy neck
Door-wards, and yon tall axe-man not behead thee,
Thou'dst hear a storm indeed!

John of Oxford:
We have heard much tumult.
Tell us, good Walter, what is it like?

Mapes:
What like?
The roll of thunder, roar of seas, and groan
Of heart-burnt mountains, crash of cataracts,
All mingled dense as the dark angel's cry
Of mutual torment; or those threatening voices
From Chaos 'gainst Creation, yell'd by night,
Which makes the firm stars tremble in their spheres.

A listener explains—

Englisht, — a mighty hubbub.

I wonder whether Darley was laughing there at his own
extravagance. Throughout the play, however, one comes
across fine disciplined images:

His Grace was very meek!

56

                                        He almost prayed!
On mouth and nose, as I have seen a Saracen!
And with what unction rare he scrubb'd the feet
Of thirteen Beggars, like a polisher
Who files the brazen toes of tarnish'd Saints
Clean-yellow.

The play was never produced. Darley made a second attempt with *Ethelstan,* which deals with the Anglo-Saxon age. Curiously enough, his brother, Charles, who later became Professor of English Literature at Queen's College, Cork, wrote a tragedy, *The Plighted Troth,* which was produced by Macready at Drury Lane in 1842. It proved a failure. I do not know whether it has ever been published.

Although Gerald Griffin won a reputation with his novels and short stories, his first ambition was to be a great dramatist. At the age of eighteen, he started to write plays and, at twenty-one, had completed four tragedies. I think that the young Limerick lad only knew the plays of Addison and Johnson. Three of the tragedies are lost but, with the last of them in his pocket, he set out for London and fame. Unfortunately, this play, *Gisippus,* was rejected, and was only staged at Drury Lane by Macready two years after Griffin's death. There was still a tradition of producing verse plays in the theatre, but times were changing, as one can see from the preface to *Gisippus,* written by a friend of Griffin's. Referring to the four plays, he wrote:

His intention was to get one of them performed at one of the great theatres, but at that time the public taste was vitiated by managers who yielded to the depraved appetite of the multitude, instead of endeavouring to correct them. Mechanical wonders, cataracts of real water, brilliant scenic representation and sights of an amphitheatricality and popular character usurped the place of legitimate drama, and, after many distressing difficulties and much valuable time sacrificed in the attempt, he gave it up as hopeless.

57

Gisippus or *The Forgotten Friend* is classical in theme and is, I think, surprisingly well-constructed, considering the poet's inexperience. The scene is Athens and Gisippus is about to marry the wealthy Sophronia. When his friend, Fulvius, arrives from Rome, he learns that his bride-to-be and Fulvius had been in love but have parted through a misunderstanding. Generously, he renounces his claim to her. After the marriage, Fulvius is suddenly recalled to Rome, unaware that Gisippus has been arrested for debt and sold into slavery. The last scenes take place in Rome outside the palace of Fulvius, who has returned in triumph from the wars. Gisippus, who has served out his term of slavery, comes to Rome, a ragged beggar. As he waits with other suppliants, he thinks that Fulvius has seen him and pretended not to know him. He then retires to a burial ground, where a duel takes place between an old friend of his, Chremos and another. Before Gisippus can stop the fight, Chremos is killed. In his despair over the supposed ingratitude of Fulvius, Gisippus stains his own sword, which he had always kept, with the blood. He is arrested and sentenced to be executed. Just in time, the real assailant confesses and Fulvius recognises the sword of his old friend. There is tension in the last scene. Will the messengers arrive in time to stay the execution? The play is rather naïve but moving. The style is thin but here and there are good lines.

> The shafts of the Boy-god ne'er wound less surely
> For being tipped with gold,

—an appropriate line, said by a friend of Fulvius, when he was about to marry the wealthy Sophronia.

Among forgotten poetic dramatists of this time was a Scotswoman, Joanna Baillie. She wrote twenty-six plays, only one of which, *De Montfort: A Tragedy*, was performed. I have the collected edition of her works published in 1851 and it runs to more than 800 pages. Her lines have little poetic value and the rhythm is stilted in movement. I confess that I could not get through many of

them. Here and there, however, can be found a good line:
> What, 'midst the dangers of eventful war,
> Still let thy mind be haunted by a woman,
> Who would, perhaps, hear of thy fall in battle,
> As Dutchmen read of earthquakes in Calabria?

James Sheridan Knowles, a Corkman, was a practical dramatist, for he had spent his early years as an actor and a few of his plays, such as *The Hunchback* and *The Love Chase* were constantly staged during the early part of the Victorian age. His technique is sure and he can give a situation in a few lines, but his verse is flat, conventional in its turn of phrase. *The Rose of Aragon* begins briskly and to the point: —

> The Prince not yet set out?
>   Not yet; he cleaves
> To home with doating on his peasant wife.
> His journey towards the frontier thrice has he
> From day to day deferred already: but
> The King, impatient of his weak delay,
> Brooks it no longer. He departs at noon.
> Guess you, my Lord, the motive of the King
> In banishing, as 'twere, at such a time,
> The Prince from Saragossa? Hard exchange
> The bridal chamber from the warrior's tent!
> The murmurings and the dalliance of love
> For the trump's braying and the clang of steel!
> Methinks, the nuptials he so interrupts
> Can scarce be to his mind.

The Hunchback, first performed at Covent Garden in 1832, picks up the Elizabethan tradition of domestic drama. The language here is equally factual but pleasant in its references: —

Julia:
>   Think not, when I am wed,
> I'll keep the house as owlet does her tower,
> Alone,—when every other bird's on wing.
> I'll use my palfrey, Helen; and my coach;

My barge, too, for excursions on the Thames;
What drives to Barnet, Hackney, Islington!
What rides to Epping, Hounslow, and Blackheath!
What sails to Greenwich, Woolwich, Fulham, Kew!
I'll set a pattern to your lady wives!

Sir Henry Taylor, 1800-1886, wrote a number of verse
plays, one of which, *Phillip van Artevelde,* about the
Belgian patriot of the thirteenth century, kept the stage,
though written in the pseudo-Elizabethan manner. It is a
fine example of horrible poetic jargon—

Why, that is bravely said. Then be it so.
Thou shalt have warranty to fight it out;
And if we're beaten, I shall stand prepared
To fly to Bruges with such as choose to follow.
And hark you! we will not go empty-handed;
We'll take a prize that's worth a good town's ransom—
A damsel whom thou wot'st of.

Charles Welles is best remembered as the friend of
Keats. In his early years, he wrote a poetic drama which
attracted no attention. Later it was discovered by Rossetti,
and Welles, encouraged by this, revised it. The complete
version was published in 1876 with an enthusiastic preface
by Swinburne. Welles had chosen a scriptural subject and
the play is entitled *Joseph and his Brethren.* The main
scenes are about Potiphar's wife, whose name was Phraxanor, and Joseph's virtuous resistance to her advances. Swinburne declared:

In the Cleopatra of Shakespeare and in the Phraxanor of
the present play there is the same imperious conscience
of power by right of supreme beauty and supreme
strength of will; the same subtle sweetness of speech;
the same delicately rendered effect of perfection in word
and gesture, never violated or made harsh even by
extreme passion.

Swinburne omits to point out that this is not, like Shakespeare's play, intended for the stage. Although some of
the scenes indeed are dramatic, in most of them the

characters speak at extreme length. Swinburne notes the
richness of the poetry; Welles was influenced a good deal
by Marlowe and by George Peele; there is also the Keatsian
note in his images: —

> Swarthy Egyptians, yellow as their gold,
> Riding on mules.

And a Shakespearean line about sunset—

> A god gigantic, habited in gold,
> Stepping from off a mount into the sea.

Here is a short scene from Act II between Phraxanor and
her Attendant:

Phrax:
> Suppose you did expect the man you love
> To wait on you about this place and time,
> What habit and behaviour would you use?

Attendant:
> Were I, like you, a lady of estate,
> I would adorn my brow with a bright star
> Of crusted diamond's lustre—stain'd with gold,
> Like to a frosted sunflower, when the morn
> Blinks in the east, and plays upon its front.
> My hair should bear a tiara of bright gems;
> And all my velvet should be loop'd about
> With colours blending into harmony.
> I would sip water fragranc'd with sweet gum,
> To give my breathing sweetness. Half reclin'd,
> I would receive him with a free discourse
> Which he should lead, wherein I'd acquiesce.

Phrax:
> Ah, child! there lies more mischief in a smile
> Than in the king's own house, and all his waste
> Of wreathed gold and weighty jewelry.—
> Come, help to dress me straight.

Attendant:
> What fashion, madam?

Phrax:
> The sultry hour well suits occasion: —

That silk of gossamer like tawny gold—
Throw it on loosely:—so, 'tis well; yet stay,—
See to the neck; fit thou some tender lace
About the rim. The precious jewel shown
But scantily is oft desired most,
And tender nets scare not the timid bird.
A little secret is a tempting thing
Beyond wide truth's confession.—Give me flowers
That I may hang them in my ample hair;
And sprinkle me with lavender and myrrh.
And wreath my arms with pearls.—So—this will do—
And in good time, for yonder Joseph comes.

Joseph certainly took a long time coming, for Phraxanor
continues her speech about him for two minutes.

Robert Browning wrote several historical tragedies and
a couple of comedies for the stage, but they have not lasted
as well as *Pippa Passes*, his lyrical play for the study. This
play consists of dramatic scenes linked together by the
soliloquies and songs of the heroine. It begins with a fine
lyrical description of dawn:

Day!
Faster and more fast,
O'er night's brim, day boils at last;
Boils, pure gold, o'er the cloud-cup's brim
Where spurting and supprest it lay—
For not a froth-flake touched the rim
Of yonder gap in the solid gray
Of the eastern cloud, an hour away!
But forth one wavelet, then another, curled,
Till the whole sunrise, not to be supprest,
Rose, reddened, and its seething breast
Flickered in bounds, grew gold, then overflowed the
world.

That is supposed to be spoken by Pippa, a young silk-
winder in the factory of a small town at Asola in northern
Italy. However, Pippa does speak more or less in character
in her other monologues. She sets out early on her one

holiday in the year, and wherever she goes, sings so happily
that those who hear her are immediately influenced for the
good. Browning was intensely interested in the problem of
good and evil, and the other characters in this play are
dire in their wickedness: one is plotting assassination; an
unfaithful wife has had her husband murdered by her
paramour, another villain is actually plotting to ensnare
Pippa herself and sell her to a rich Englishman. Here is a
much quoted song of Pippa which everyone knows, in its
dramatic setting. Ottima, the wife, and her German lover
speak: —

Ottima:

Crown me your Queen, your spirit's arbitress,
Magnificent in sin. Say that!

Sebald:

                  I crown you
My great white queen, my spirit's arbitress,
Magnificent . . .

(*From without is heard the voice of Pippa, singing*)

The year's at the spring,
The day's at the morn;
Morning's at seven;
The hill-side's dew-pearled;
The lark's on the wing;
The snail's on the thorn;
God's in his heaven—
All right's with the world!

(*Pippa passes*)

Sebald:

God's in his heaven! Do you hear that? Who spoke?
You, you spoke!

Ottima:

                Oh — that little ragged girl!
She must have rested on the step: we give them
But this one holiday the whole year round.
Did you ever see our silk-mills—their inside?
There are ten silk-mills now belonging to you.

She stoops to pick my double heartsease . . . Sh!
She does not hear: call you out louder!
Sebald:

         Leave me!
Go, get your clothes on—dress those shoulders!
Ottima:
 Sebald?
Sebald:
 Wipe off that paint. I hate you!
The revulsion seems very sudden but this play is really an
allegory. Lennox Robinson told me that *Pippa Passes* was
produced here on the stage once by a dramatic society and
proved effective.

 Robert Browning began with two long narrative monologues, *Paracelsus* and *Sordello*. His interest in the actual
theatre was due to a chance meeting with the great actor-
manager, Macready, who asked him to write a play for
him. He chose a historical subject, Wentworth, Earl of
Strafford, his rise and fall from power. Following the
declining tradition of acting verse plays, Browning wrote
in a plain unfigurative style, conversational in tendency.
Here are a few sarcastic lines by Pym to his rival, Strafford: the latter is waiting to see King Charles and meets
Pym.
Pym: I
 Think always of you, Wentworth.
Wentworth:

         The old voice!
 I wait the king, sir.
Pym:

       True — you look so pale!
 A Council sits within; when that breaks up
 He'll see you.
Wentworth:
 Sir, I thank you.
Pym:

      Oh, thank Laud!

You know when Laud once gets on Church affairs
The case is desperate: he'll not be long
To-day: he only means to prove, to-day,
We English all are mad to have a hand
In butchering the Scots for serving God
After their fathers' fashion: only that!
Wentworth:
Sir, keep your jests for those who relish them!
Macready altered, cut and re-arranged the play for the stage and it was a moderate success.

Of the other plays, the best liked was *A Blot in the Scutcheon,* a tragedy of young love and death, which was greatly admired by Dickens. Professor Dowden points out that certain passages in it are almost ludicrously undramatic owing to the long speeches and delayed action.

If Romeo before he flung up his ladder of ropes had paused, like Mertoun, to salute his mistress with a tender morceau from the opera, it is to be feared that old Capulet would have come upon the scene in his night-gown, prepared to hasten the catastrophe with a long sword.

But Dowden admits that *A Blot in the Scutcheon,* with its breadth of outline, its striking situations, and its mastery of the elementary passions of love and wrath and pride and pity—gives us assurance that Browning might have taken a place of considerable distinction had he been born in an age of great dramatic poetry. However, after a few years, he lost interest in the stage and returned to his monologues, in which he analysed human motives and states of mind. Nevertheless his dramatic experience must have been of value to him and in the stage plays one finds hints of the abrupt eccentric rhythms which were to become a mark of his style.

In 1860, the young Swinburne published two verse plays, *The Queen Mother,* which deals with the massacre of St. Bartholomew's Eve; and *Rosamond,* which tells the tragedy of the unfortunate mistress of Henry II, whose sad fate was mourned in many of the old ballads. Rosamond was the *femme fatale* who was to dominate the later plays of Swinburne. She describes herself—

> Yea, I am found the woman in all tales,
> The face caught always in the story's face;
> I Helen, holding Paris by the lips,
> Smote Hector through the head; I Cressida
> So kissed men's mouths that they went sick or mad,
> Stung right at brain with me; I Guenevere
> Made my queen's eyes so precious and my hair
> Delicate with such gold in its soft ways
> And my mouth honied so for Launcelot.

The volume attracted no attention. 'Of all still-born books', wrote Swinburne, 'it was the stillest'. Five years later came *Atalanta in Calydon,* with which the poet won immediate fame. This lyrical play for the study is classical in theme. The goddess Artemis, better known as Diana, angered by the neglect of her altars in Calydon, sends a mighty boar into the country. Meleager, the King's son, is in love with the beautiful virgin Atalanta, who was, as you remember, a famous runner. Meleager kills the boar and presents the spoils to Atalanta. His two uncles, who had been unsuccessful in the hunt, try to wrest the spoils from her and Meleager slays them. Queen Althaea, his mother, has a magic brand on which his life depends: enraged by the death of her brothers, she casts it into the fire and Meleager dies. Poetically the play is a novel blend of the classical and the romantic or pre-Raphaelite style. Many of the speeches are long and that of the dying Meleager runs to more than a hundred lines. Then we get one of those classically compressed replies which occur in this play. The grief-stricken Atalanta speaks only two lines—

> Hail thou: but I with heavy face and feet
> Turn homeward and am gone out of thine eyes.

The play is best known for its wonderful choric lyrics, some of which are to be found in all anthologies—this one, for instance—

When the hounds of spring are on winter's traces,
The mother of months in meadow or plain
Fills the shadows and windy places
With lisp of leaves and ripple of rain;
And the brown bright nightingale amorous
Is half assuaged for Itylus,
For the Thracian ships and the foreign faces,
The tongueless vigil, and all the pain.

and it moves rapidly, rhythmically—

Where shall we find her, how shall we sing to her,
Fold our hands round her knees, and cling?
O, that man's heart were as fire and could spring to
her,
Fire, or the strength of the streams that spring!
For the stars and the winds are unto her
As raiment, as songs of the harp-player;
For the risen stars and the fallen cling to her,
And the south-west wind and the west wind sing.

In the last wonderful lyric interchanged between the chorus
and the protagonist, one can hear, despite the lyric speed,
the rhythm of drums.

Atalanta:

I would that with feet
Unsandalled, unshod,
Overbold, overfleet,
I had swum not nor trod
From Arcadia to Calydon northward, a blast of the
envy of God.

Meleager:

Unto each man his fate;
Unto each as he saith
In whose fingers the weight
Of the world is as breath;
Yet I would that in clamour of battle mine hands had
laid hold upon death.

Chorus:

Not with cleaving of shields

67

And their clash in thine ear,
When the lord of fought fields
Breaketh spearshaft from spear,
Thou art broken, our lord, thou art broken, with
travail and labour and fear.

Soon after the publication of this classical drama, Swinburne published *Chastelard,* the first of his lengthy trilogy of plays on the life of Mary Queen of Scots. Here again is the *femme fatale* : in the words of Chastelard—

I know her ways of loving, all of them;
A sweet soft way the first is; afterward
It burns and bites like fire; the end of that,
Charred dust, and eyelids bitten through with smoke.

The poetry is pre-Raphaelite in manner, sensuous, musical and smooth. Now some lines from the fifth Act, in which Mary bids farewell for ever to Scotland—

Seven years since
Did I take leave of my fair land of France,
My joyous mother, mother of my joy,
Weeping; and now with many a woe between
And space of seven years' darkness, I depart
From this distempered and unnatural earth
That casts me out unmothered, and go forth
On this grey sterile bitter gleaming sea
With neither tears nor laughter, but a heart
That from the softest temper of its blood
Is turned to fire and iron.

Swinburne wrote a number of other blank verse tragedies on the Elizabethan model but in his own individual style, remarkable for its facile flow and sheer verbalism.

The dream of a great epoch of verse-drama went on. At the age of sixty-six, the Poet Laureate, yielding to a suggestion of the actor manager, Henry Irving, began to write historical tragedies and on such themes as Harold, Queen Mary, Becket. *Harold* appeared in 1877 and here are the opening lines. Aldwyth, the future queen, and some courtiers are watching a comet.

1st Courtier:
Lo! there once more—this is the seventh night!
Yon grimly-glaring, treble-brandish'd scourge
Of England!
2nd Courtier: Horrible!
1st Courtier:
Look you, there's a star
That dances in it as mad with agony!
3rd Courtier:
Ay, like a spirit in Hell who skips and flies
To right and left, and cannot escape the flame.
2nd Courtier:
Steam'd upward from the undescendible
Abysm.
1st Courtier:
Or floated downward from the throne
Of God Almighty.
Aldwyth:
Gamel, son of Orm,
What thinkest thou this means?
Gamel: War, my dear lady!
Aldwyth: Doth this affright thee?
Gamel: Mightily, my dear lady!
Aldwyth:
Stand by me, then, and look upon my face
Not on the comet.

This indication of Aldwyth's courage is a fine stroke. One thinks at once, though, of the omens in Shakespeare's *Julius Caesar*. Actually Tennyson wrote the lines on observing a comet from his country house at Farringford. I saw the play many years ago at the Court Theatre at Sloan's Square, London, and thought it very dramatic. But being used to the violent, heavily-imaged speech of the Plantagenets in Shakespeare's Chronicle plays, I felt that the smooth Tennysonian lines were too mild for Harold, William the Bastard and their ferocious warriors. Tennyson may have got the suggestion for his Becket play from

George Darley's tragedy. With Henry Irving in the leading
part, this play by Tennyson was successful. The last scene,
with its touch of Elizabethan rhetoric, is certainly exciting—

Monks:

Here is the great Archbishop! He lives! He lives!

Becket:

Together? get you back! go on with the office.

Monks:

Come, then, with us to vespers.

Becket:

How can I come
When you so block the entry? Back, I say!
Go on with the office. Shall not Heaven be served
Tho' earth's last earthquake clash'd the minster-bells
And the great deeps were broken up again,
And hiss'd against the sun?

Comparison between the Becket of Darley, Tennyson and
T. S. Eliot in our own time would be interesting as a thesis.
Eliot's play, which was intended as a pageant in Canterbury Cathedral, was arranged for the stage by the producer Martin Brown. Although the American poet was a
convert to Anglicanism and a declared Royalist, he evokes
for us the intense religious passion of the protagonist
directly—and indirectly in the chorus of the Poor Women
of Canterbury. When we have read it, we feel that Darley
and Tennyson were merely treating a rather interesting
historical theme with the respect due to it.

A lesser-known poet who has been attracting attention
in the last few years is John Davidson. He was a member
of the Rhymers' Club and always walked out when Yeats
came in. In the eighties, as a Scottish schoolmaster, he
wrote a number of verse dramas, including a five-act blank
verse chronicle play about Bruce, and an equally long
pastoral play in the Elizabethan manner. One of his plays
was experimental for he chose a contemporary theme and
contemporary language and so anticipated a problem which
T. S. Eliot, W. H. Auden and others have tried to solve in

our time. The play is called *Smith,* or, in other words, Everyman, and Davidson was well aware of the difficulties, for his hero says:—

Our language is too worn, too much abused,
Jaded and over-spurred, wind-broken, lame —
The hackneyed roadster every bagman mounts.
I cannot tell you what I want.

Unfortunately the play is not well constructed because there are two antagonists: a despairing poet, who speaks in a lofty declamatory manner, and Smith, who shares with the poet the same hatred of modern economic and social conditions. Smith falls in love with the daughter of a wealthy man and the action culminates in the last act when they both climb a mountain with the intention of throwing themselves from a cliff. At the top they find the body of the poet who has just committed suicide by cutting his wrists. They are pursued by father and friends, who capture the girl and lead her off stage. Smith follows and, by means which are not revealed to us, recaptures his beloved. Enter father and friend again just as Smith, with a final brief speech, clasps Magdalen in his arms and leaps over the brink. The play is called a tragic farce. I do not think the poet wanted the audience to laugh at this melodramatic ending, but I fear they would do so.

Michael Field, the pen-name of two spinster ladies, steadily wrote a series of historical tragedies in five acts and in blank verse.

Lastly two Irish verse dramatists. The first is Oscar Wilde, who, at the beginning of his career, wrote a poetic tragedy, hoping that the part of the heroine might attract a celebrated American actress. Its title is *The Duchess of Padua* and, as you probably guess, it was a close imitation of Webster's *Duchess of Malfi.* Many years ago, I saw it performed by a small professional group who gave several seasons of drama in the Irish Trade Union's Hall in Capel Street. Some of the scenes were effective but the play moved slowly and when the fifth act started, the time was coming up to 11 o'clock. I began to worry for I was living outside Dublin at the time and had to catch the last train to Killiney. The dying Duchess sat up and made a long speech and I thought the play was drawing to a close but in a minute she sat up again and began to make another speech. I left my seat in the front and tip-toed down the central aisle. I thought I heard stealthy sounds and glanced back. To my horror, I found that the entire audience was creeping out after me.

The other Irish poet dramatist is John Todhunter, a Dublin doctor, who retired to London to devote himself to poetry. During the 'eighties, he wrote a number of plays on Greek and romantic themes, several of which were performed by the new Independent Theatre, where Florence Farr was a producer. In his full-length drama, *Tristram and Iseult,* he cleverly varied the legend for dramatic purposes. Todhunter turned from long to short verse plays. His best short play is *The Poison Flower,* which is drawn from a short story by Hawthorne. It takes place in Padua during the latter half of the fifteenth century. Giovanni, a student, rents an apartment and as he enters it, he hears the lovely voice of a girl singing in the next garden and, looking from his window, sees Beatrice, the daughter of the mysterious Dr. Rappaccini. The garden he sees is strange for it is full of exotic shrubs and flowers. The whole mood of the play approaches that of the *Fin de Siècle.* Rappaccini, in his experiments, has nurtured his daughter on deadly poisons; even her breath can wither flowers. Needless to say, she and Giovanni fall in love. The theme is allegorical: can true love overcome evil?

This short play and others were produced in the private theatre of a club at Bedford Park, where Todhunter lived. Nearby had come to live a young Irish poet, who became friendly with the middle-aged writer and must have seen his plays. Need I say who it was?—W. B. Yeats. I have always fancied that this was the beginning of modern Irish verse drama. Consciously or not, Yeats realised that in order to start again, it was necessary to break from the stale Victorian convention of five-act pseudo-Elizabethan tragedies and, in a humble way, be content with lyric plays in one act.

Yeats's Early Plays

As a youth, Yeats became interested in lyrical drama probably owing to the influence of Shelley. *The Island of Statues* appeared in the *Dublin University Review* in 1885 when he was just twenty. It is an Arcadian play and the island is ruled by an enchantress, an idea probably borrowed from Shelley's *Witch of Atlas*. It was never republished, but one delightful lyric from it, 'The Cloak, the Boat and the Shoes' appeared in his first collection of poems. In the same year *Mosada*, a dramatic poem of his, was published privately by his father. It takes place in mediaeval Spain in a dungeon of the Spanish Inquisition, in which the young heroine, a Moorish girl, is held prisoner and is about to be burned when her plight is discovered by her Christian lover. It is naïve but shows, I think, the dramatic gift. The proud father of the poet presented a copy to Father Gerard Manley Hopkins, a lecturer in the Catholic University here—not a very tactful gift. The young English convert disliked the play and when the two met, they were very cool to each other. I have often wondered what would have happened if they had become friends. Hopkins, in an astonishing way, anticipated the modern poetry of our century. Had Yeats been influenced by him, our literary revival might have been different.

When Yeats went to live in London, he met Maud Gonne and his love for her inspired his first real play, *The Countess Cathleen*. As I mentioned in my last lecture, he was a neighbour of the older Irish poet, John Todhunter, and saw some of his plays at a small club theatre in Bedford Park. In one of them Florence Farr acted the principal part and he was inspired by her beautiful speaking of verse. I suggest that Yeats was encouraged by the example of Todhunter to write directly for the stage. *The Countess Cathleen*, though not a full-length play, was the longest one he ever wrote and, consciously or not, the one-act verse plays which Todhunter wrote may have caused him to break with the Victorian convention of the five-act tragedy. He mentions in his Memoirs that he had seen *The Cenci* and Tennyson's *Becket* and had reacted from their declamatory tone as he had reacted from the declamatory style of the Young Ireland school. *The Countess Cathleen* was published in 1892, a confused version. I remember vaguely one scene in which all the traditional sidhe, shee-ogues, cluricans, and spooks assembled. Over eight years and more Yeats continued to change and revise this play. In one of the scenes, the Countess calls in her Steward to give her an inventory of her property. You will find the same situation in Webster's *Duchess of Malfi,* and I think Yeats had this play in mind as a model. Certainly all the critics have had the same idea for they all insist that the play lacks dramatic conflict.

In the forties I was associated with a voluntary group, the Lyric Theatre Company, which included well-known professional as well as semi-professional actors, and we hired the Abbey Theatre on Sunday nights to put on verse plays. The plays of Yeats had almost disappeared from his own theatre and we began with *The Countess Cathleen,* which had not been seen for seventeen years. I discussed the play with a very clever woman, a friend of mine, who said that there was no conflict because the Countess Cathleen acted like a real woman and, having once made up her mind to save her people from famine at all costs, did so. In other words, the play was beyond the convention of ordinary tragedy. We followed that idea and the leading part was played by that fine actress, Eithne Dunne, and it was deeply moving and for us a great success. Yeats theorised a great deal in essays about his own poetry but said little about his plays. Had he realised that he was approaching drama from a different angle in his first play and said so, he might have attracted more critical attention. But he did not know what he was doing for in later years he wrote in *Dramatis Personae*:

'The Countess sells her soul, but she is not transformed. If I were to think out that scene to-day, she would at the moment her hand has signed burst into loud laughter, mock at all that she has held holy, horrify the peasants in the midst of their temptations. Nothing satisfied me but Florence Farr's performance in the part of Aleel ... and after five-and-thiry years, I keep among my unforgettable memories the sense of coming disaster she put into the words:

                                                But now
     Two grey horned owls hooted above our heads'.
Despite the writer of the play, let us take the opening lines from the 1900 version which we used:
Mary:
     What can have made the grey hen flutter so?
Teig:
     They say that now the land is famine struck
     The graves are walking.
Mary:
                         There is something that the hen hears.
Teig:
     And that is not the worst; at Tubber-vanach
     A woman met a man with ears spread out,
     And they moved up and down like a bat's wing.
Mary:
     What can have kept your father all this while?
Teig:
     Two nights ago, at Carrick-orus churchyard,
     A herdsman met a man who had no mouth,
     He saw him plainly by the light of the moon.
     Nor eyes, nor ears; his face a wall of flesh;
Mary:
     Look out, and tell me if your father's coming.
Teig:
     Mother!
Mary:
          What is it?

Teig:
                                    In the bush beyond,
There are two birds—if you can call them birds—
I could not see them rightly for the leaves.
But they've the shape and colour of horned owls
And I'm half certain they've a human face.

Dramatically this is surely effective; the speech is simple
and yet imaginative, the dialect is delicately suggested. Or
take the higher level on which the main characters speak.
The Countess, turning from Aleel and speaking almost to
herself, and then turning back to him—

                                    He bids me go
Where none of mortal creatures but the swan
Dabbles, and there you would pluck the harp, when
the trees
Had made a heavy shadow about our door,
And talk among the rustling of the reeds,
When night hunted the foolish sun away
With stillness and pale tapers. No—no—no!
I cannot. Although I weep, I do not weep
Because that life would be most happy, and here
I find no way, no end. Nor do I weep
Because I had longed to look upon your face,
But that a night of prayer has made me weary.

When one compares this mode of speech, seemingly natural
and yet lyrical, with the pseudo-Elizabethan style of most
Victorian verse drama, one is tempted to find in it something new and fresh. Ironically enough, the play was first
acted at the Vice-regal Lodge in Dublin and then later by
the newly formed Irish National Theatre Company.

   Yeats had less difficulty with his second lyrical play in
one act, *The Land of Heart's Desire,* which was produced
in London in 1894 and became very popular with dramatic
societies and in schools. It is a simple theme: a young
bride lured away by a fairy child, and it has that haunting
refrain through it—

The wind blows out of the gates of the day,
The wind blows over the lonely of heart,
And the lonely of heart is withered away.

Later, in his short patriotic drama, *Kathleen ni Houlihan,*
Yeats reversed the theme: the young bridegroom is drawn
away by the Shan Van Vocht. When I saw *The Land of
Heart's Desire* for the first time in the Abbey, the fairy
child was a big bouncing girl of about sixteen and as she
leaped onto the stage, it shook.

A.E., who was inclined to repeat himself, often told me
of a great romantic play which Yeats dreamed about when
they were both students at the School of Art in Dublin. A
world-weary sea-captain, who wants to escape from himself, captures a galley on which there is a beautiful queen.
He gains her love by a magic spell but then realises that
this love is but the reflection of himself so he sails away
into the Unknown. Later whenever Yeats mentioned it to
him, A.E. told me, the play seemed to lose its mysterious
attraction, its beauty. This play was *The Shadowy Waters,*
and in *The Irish Renaissance,* a collection of essays, published recently by the Dolmen Press, David Clark has
written an essay, in which he gives examples of the many
drafts and re-writings of this play. Yeats was about to
publish it in 1896 and hesitated. In that year the French
poet-dramatist, Rostand, published a play called *La Prin-
cesse Lointaine.* It also begins on board a ship. The trouba-
dour, Rudolf, who had fallen in love with a lady of Tripoli
whom he had never seen, is journeying to her court. This
is a direct dramatic play and Rostand had the advantage
of being able to draw on the poems of the Troubadours.
Yeats had no such advantage for his dream play. It was
printed at last in 1900, staged in 1904, re-written in 1906
when Synge was already a coming force. It was the epitome
of the Celtic Twilight. And there was one great change. In
all the printed versions, the hero and the heroine do not
part; they both sail towards the Unknown. All the critics
say the play was unactable and Ernest Boyd wrote of it:

'The dramatic claims of the play may be said never to have existed; from the earliest to the latest version the theme remains fundamentally incapable of dramatic expression.'

Eliot waved it away as 'pretty piece of pre-Raphaeliteism'. Yeats himself surrendered and he included it as only a dramatic poem; you will find it not in the *Collected Plays* but in the *Collected Poems*. I saw it played on the Abbey stage but at the age of seventeen I could not judge it: nevertheless, I still think that, as a period piece, given the right actors, the right voices, the right audience, it could hold the attention, provided the 1900 text were used. In the later version a later run of images are mingled. The late Dr. Catherine Spurgeon discovered that the imagery in Shakespeare's plays has an underlying subconscious unity. In re-writing *The Shadowy Waters*, so often, Yeats lost that unity. Boyd tells us that the following lines are the *leitmotiv* of the poet's early poetry and philosophy, when Forgael says—

All would be well
Could we but give us wholly to the dreams,
And get into their world that to the sense
Is shadow, and not linger wretchedly
Among substantial things: for it is dreams
That lift us to the flowing, changing world
That the heart longs for. What is love itself,
Even though it be the lightest of light love,
But dreams that hurry from beyond the world
To make low laughter more than meat and drink,
Though it but set us sighing? Fellow-wanderer,
Could we but mix ourselves into a dream,
Not in its image on the mirror!

And the lyric intensity increases—

I've had teachers.
Aengus and Edain ran up out of the wave—
You'd never doubt that it was life they promised
Had you looked on them face to face as I did,

79

With so red lips, and running on such feet,
And having such wide-open, shining eyes.

Consider this. At the age of forty-one Yeats was still pondering over an adolescent dream. Perhaps Professor Ellman was right and Yeats did not come of age until he reached his fiftieth year.

St. John Irvine, who was manager of the Abbey Theatre for some time, tells us in his reminiscences an amusing story of a production of *The Shadowy Waters*. It was at the time when limes were still used and during a light rehearsal, Yeats was sitting in the stalls as various effects were tried with the lime-lights. They were unsatisfactory until suddenly the stage was filled with an exquisite ethereal hue, and the poet exclaimed: 'That's right. Hold it. Hold it!' and a voice came from the ladder, 'I can't, Mr. Yeats, the blasted thing is on fire.'

By 1900 Yeats was back in Dublin and soon was in the midst of much dramatic activity. You all know how the National Theatre was founded with the help of the two actors, the brothers Fay, and then later the Abbey Theatre. Yeats wrote not only verse plays but prose plays also: such as the one-act *Kathleen ni Houlihan*, in which Lady Gregory had a share. He collaborated with George Moore in *Diarmuid and Grania*, which was played at the Gaiety. It was not published but a young English graduate some years ago discovered a copy of the script and it was published in the *Dublin Magazine*. You can deduce, I think, by the images the passages written by Yeats. Both collaborated in another play about a mystic, *Where there is Nothing*, but quarrelled over it and later Yeats re-wrote it as *The Unicorn from the Stars*. Many years later, in a vigorous poem which looks like a sonnet but has only thirteen lines, 'The Fascination of what's Difficult', Yeats wrote, referring to the winged horse which he had neglected—

My curse on plays
That have to be set up in fifty ways,

On the day's war with every knave and dolt,
Theatre business, management of men.
I swear before the dawn comes round again
I'll find the stable and pull out the bolt.

And now to come back to the verse plays of this period.
Did practical experience, the fact that he had, lucky poet,
a theatre of his own, help his technique? I would say certainly. But I would suggest that his method of chanting
his verse while composing slowed down the rhythm. Also
his aloof temperament added a difficulty. In illustration
there is another amusing story told by St. John Irvine.
Yeats was moving absentmindedly in the scene-dock one
day when a young lady, in passing, said, 'Good day, Mr.
Yeats.' He stopped and asked, 'Who are you?' She replied,
'Oh, Mr. Yeats, I am playing the leading rôle in your play
this week.'

In several of these early plays Yeats began to develop his
theme of Cuchulain, which was to last for the rest of his
life. His plays have not the strong quality of the sagas, but
they do reflect another quality in them. The late Robin
Flower, an English poet and fine Gaelic scholar, wrote in
his book, *The Irish Tradition,* that the men of the sagas
had an exquisite sensitiveness to external impressions. He
took in illustration an episode from the Táin Bó Fraích, a
tale perhaps of the eighth century. Queen Maeve and her
husband Ailill have instructed Fraoch, son of a fairy
woman and the lover of their daughter, Findabhair, to
swim in a monster-haunted pool. He is about to leave the
water unharmed when Ailill bids him back: " 'Come not
out of the water,' said Ailill, 'until thou bring me a branch
from yonder rowan tree on the river's brink. For its berries
are beautiful to me.' " Fraoch returns and breaks a branch
from the tree and brings it on his back across the water.
"And Findabhair cried out: 'Is that not beautiful to see?'
For beautiful it was to her to see Fraoch over the dark
water, the body so white, the hair so lovely, the face so
shapely, the eye of deep grey, and all the tender youth

faultless and without blame, his face narrow below and broad above, his straight and flawless make, the branch with the crimson berries between the throat and the white face." In the words of Dr. Flower: 'that vision so clearly seen, so surely and swiftly rendered is of the very heart of the saga literature.'

On Baile's Strand appeared in 1904 and its theme is that tragic story which tells how Cuchulain slew his own son of whose birth he had not known. Here is an example of what one may call lyrical eloquence in which the rhythm is rightly speeded. Cuchulain is talking of Aoife actually the mother of his son—

Ah! Conchubar, had you seen her
With that high, laughing, turbulent head of hers
Thrown backward, and the bowstring at her ear,
Or sitting at the fire with those grave eyes
Full of good counsel as it were with wine,
Or when love ran through all the lineaments
Of her wild body—although she had no child,
None other had all beauty, queen or lover,
Or was so fitted to give birth to kings.

'Lineaments' was, of course, a favourite word of William Blake. And note the impressionistic method of description—

The head grows prouder in the light of the dawn,
And friendship thickens in the murmuring dark
Where the spare hazels meet the wool-white foam.

or again—

Out of the cold dark of the rich sea.

Note also the plainness of many of the images: Cuchulain speaking about his enemies to the unknown young man—

But I'd need no avenger. You and I
Would scatter them like water from a dish.

Even unsympathetic critics admit that the last scene is dramatic. The Blind Man and the Fool have crept into the Assembly Hall and are sitting on a bench. Cuchulain enters, after slaying Connla, and overhears what they are saying—

Blind Man:
  Somebody is trembling, Fool! The bench is shaking.
  Why are you trembling? Is Cuchulain going to hurt
  us? It was not I who told you, Cuchulain.
Fool:
  It is Cuchulain who is trembling. It is Cuchulain who
  is shaking the bench.
Blind Man:
  It is his own son he has slain.

Padraic Colum, in a rather stern essay entitled 'A Poet's
Progress in the Theatre', published in 'The Dublin Magazine' in 1936, suggests that there is a weakness in the play.
Cuchulain, who liked the young man, suddenly fights him
because of the 'witches of the air'. In the original saga, the
young man, in ignorance that the great hero is his father,
taunts him and dares him to fight. When he is dead,
Cuchulain recognises on his hand the red gold ring of
Aoife. Mr. Colum may indeed be right but the Witches of
the Air, or, if you like, Morrigu, the war goddess and the
Irish Furies, the daughters of Cailitin, constantly drove
Cuchulain into an excess of violence. However, Padraic
Colum does note the dramatic conflict in the play though
he diminishes it to a wrangle:
  '*On Baile's Strand* is a wrangle from beginning to end:
  the Fool and the Blind Man who are the shadows of
  Cuchulain and Conchubhar wrangle, Cuchulain and
  Conchubhar wrangle, the Young Man and Cuchulain
  wrangle; Cuchulain himself is so unstable that one feels
  he has a perpetual wrangle with himself. The wrangle
  goes on after the death of the Young Man for the Fool
  and the Blind Man resume theirs. The play has the
  impressiveness of a thing that has inherent character. In
  Yeats's development as a writer of a high kind of poetic
  eloquence this play is the peak.'
You may have noticed that these plays of the Middle
period, *On Baile's Strand, The King's Threshold, Deirdre,*

all observe the three unities, probably because they are in one act without different scenes, and the story is taken at its crisis I do not think Yeats was much interested in that text book, 'Aristotle's Poetics'. Yeats has acknowledged that his play, *The King's Threshold*, published in 1904, was suggested by *Sancan,* a play by Edwin Ellis, published in 1896, with whom he collaborated in his editing of Blake. I read *Sancan* in our National Library and the copy may still be there. It is written in heroic rhyming couplets and has some good lines but the atmosphere is not Irish. Perhaps Yeats had suggested the theme to Ellis. Certainly later he followed very carefully its structure and technique. Both plays are interesting for the main character is static. I fancy that Yeats or his friend found the story in Lady Wilde's *Tales and Legends,* a book which Yeats used much as a source. I do not know whether Sancan was the original pronunciation in Irish. Dr. George Sigerson once told me that in ancient Irish there was no aspiration. The question of pronunciation in the early days of the revival was a problem. Thomas MacDonagh once told me that Yeats had come round to his house one evening to ask for the correct pronunciation of the name of the Hound of Ulster. MacDonagh, using all the gutturals, said 'Cuchulain', and Yeats, much alarmed, said, 'I thought it was Coolin.' He was not completely wrong for a range of wild precipitous mountains in the Isle of Skye are known as the Coolins. The island was ruled by Scatach and Cuchulain came there for a course in military tactics.

The King's Threshold deals with the old Irish custom of the 'sit-down' and of the hunger strike. In the original version which I saw several times, the chief bard wins back the poetic privileges. It is Yeats's own belief, proclaiming a poet's place in society and the play caused much offence and was sneered at because of this claim. As you know, after the tragic death of Terence MacSwiney, he altered the play and most critics prefer the tragic ending. Padraic Colum wrote of the first version :

'A poet in so triumphant a role is not a sympathetic personage; the play that had such an ending was not poignant. But in the new version Seanchan dies, and his death gives rise to solemn poetry.'

That may be so but the other version is more in accordance with the great and powerful bardic tradition. I have never forgotten my thrill as a student when I first heard the words Seanchan addressed to the young girl:

> The mothers that have borne you mated rightly,
> They'd little ears as thirsty as your ears
> For many love songs. Go to the young men.
> Are not the ruddy flesh and the thin flanks
> And the broad shoulders worthy of desire?
> Go from me! Here is nothing for your eyes.
> But it is I that am singing you away—
> Singing you to the young men.

The 'ruddy flesh' comes from Blake. Yeats does not mention that the strange reference to leprosy was borrowed by him from his friend's play. You remember how Seanchan turns to the young Princesses at the end of the speech and says—

> There's no sound hand among you—no sound hand.
> Away with you! away with all of you!
> You are all lepers! There is leprosy
> Among the plates and dishes that you have carried.
> And wherefore have you brought me leper's wine?

And the image develops in his delirium—

> Where did I say the leprosy had come from?
> I said it came from a leper's hand,

(Enter Cripples)

> And that he walked the highway. But that's folly,
> For he was walking up there in the sky.
> And there he is even now, with his white hand
> Thrust out of the blue air, and blessing them
> With leprosy.

First Cripple:

> He's pointing at the moon

That's coming out up yonder, and he calls it
Leprous, because the daylight whitens it.
Seanchan:
He's holding up his hand above them all—
King, noblemen, princesses—blessing all.
Who could imagine he'd have so much patience?

When I saw the play many years ago I was surprised
the moment I went into the theatre. Let me picture that
famous theatre for you. The procenium and the woodwork
were painted black, the walls were light brown or stone
colour and the two walls, left and right, had each an orna-
mented gilt shield. On the left were steps which led to a
stage door, known as Lady Gregory's door. That night I
saw new steps near it leading up to the stage. When the
house lights went down, an old man in a white night-gown
with a peaked night-cap came feebly down the stairs, holding a lighted candle and then went up the new steps to the
stage and spoke to us about the play. This Prologue was
never printed, but a few years ago I happened to mention it
in an article and a dramatic critic, who had been elevated
to the Abbey Board, wrote to the paper and said that Mr.
Clarke, as usual, was yielding to his imagination. I was
certain I had seen that old man but how could I prove it?
Happily the Secretary of the Abbey Theatre examined the
files and found that I was right and the new Director, to
give him his due, apologised. Now Yeats wasted nothing;
in his very last play, 1939, that old man appears again as
Prologue. But like Yeats himself, he had changed and his
language was not as nice, for he says to the audience:

'If there are more, I beg them not to shuffle their feet or
talk when the actors are speaking. I am sure that as I
am producing a play for people I like, it is not probable,
in this vile age, that they will be more in number than
those who listened to the first performance of Milton's
Comus. On the present occasion they must know the old
epics and Mr. Yeats's plays about them: such people,
however poor, have libraries of their own. If there are

more than a hundred I won't be able to escape people who are educating themselves out of the Book Societies and the like, sciolists all, pickpockets and opinionated bitches. Why pickpockets? I will explain that, I will make it all quite clear....
Drums and pipe behind the scene.
That's from the musicians; I asked them to do that if I was getting excited.'

The imaginative story of Deirdre became a sort of challenge to the revivalists. Ferguson had written a short rather dull dramatic version—interesting in its technique, which Bulmer Hobson believed to anticipate that of radio drama: it consists of a sequence of scenes in different places, fading in and fading out. A.E., in one of the first plays of the movement, chose the theme; Synge wrote on it; the neglected Herbert Trench gave us an epic narrative; James Stephens, a happy prose romance of Deirdre's early years. Yeats prepared slowly for his task. I suspect that he regarded it at the time as his opus magnus, and he must have been disappointed at the reaction, summarised later by Ernest Boyd. He notes the advance in Yeats's command of stage effects but concludes:

'Were it not that the subject is the crisis of a tragedy Deirdre, Naisi and Conchubar would be but the poetic expression of a symbolist's reverie, as he turns the pages of Ireland's legendary history.'

A modern critic of the 1930's, Louis MacNeice, dismissing the early plays with the customary impatience, described *Deirdre* as one of the early tapestry-like fantasies, and he quotes Yeats's own words, written in 1899:

'The theatre began in ritual, and it cannot come to its greatness again without recalling words to their ancient sovereignty.'

Yeats always believed this but in 1904 he had become a practical dramatist. In this play we have three women musicians as narrators taken from the Greek convention, but showing us one reason why Yeats was attracted later by the similar figures in the Noh plays. The action is carefully contrived; all moves towards the inevitable climax. The poetic rhythm is slowed down, giving perhaps a tranced effect; only in a lyric of the Musicians is there that lighter rhythm of the early plays: simple words, and yet so evocative:—

'Why is it,' Queen Edain said,
'If I do but climb the stair
To the tower overhead,
Where the winds are calling there,
Or the gannets calling out
In waste places of the sky,
There's so much to think about
That I cry, that I cry?'

The setting of this anachronistic lyric, a tower by the sea, was suggested by a play of Maeterlinck. The atmosphere is intensified by the references to an older love-story with the same tragic ending. No doubt the action is stilled as the lovers, who know they are doomed, play chess. But underneath there is concentrated emotion when Deirdre suddenly stops and says:

I cannot go on playing like that woman
That had the cold blood of the sea in her veins.

And Naoise replies—

It is your move. Take up your man again.

Critics then and ever since tell us that Deirdre and Naoise talk of themselves as legendary figures and think of their future fame. And that is so. She says to the Musicians—

Women, if I die,
If Naoise die this night, how will you praise?
What words seek out? for that will stand to you;
For being but dead we shall have many friends.
All through your wanderings, the doors of kings
Shall be thrown wider open, the poor man's hearth
Heaped with new turf, because you are wearing this
(*Gives Musician a bracelet*)
To show that you have Deirdre's story right.

88

But in actual history many heroes have been aware of their future fame. It has been a poetic convention. In Pope's spendid poem, 'Heloise and Abelard', Heloise commits their sorrow to future ages. In real life heroes and patriots have identified themselves with a cause and hoped to be remembered with it in the future. Take those famous words of Emmet: 'Let no man write my epitaph.'

Many critics tell us that Naoise would not have been so simple as to walk into the trap prepared for him and that the wily old Conchubar would not have let Deirdre to mourn over the corpse, but would guess that she had a knife concealed. But poetic drama is not realistic. The audience will accept stage effects as Shakespeare well knew. On one occasion, the verse dramatist, Gordon Bottomley gave me a play of his to read. I noticed a discrepancy in it and, rather nervously, wrote to him about it. He replied:

'I am glad you noticed that discrepancy but it was quite deliberate. I wanted a certain stage effect and I knew that the audience at this emotional point, would not notice it.'

For an example of the Yeatsian chant used with dramatic effect, we have the lament of the Women Musicians, that twilight chanting which fascinated so many when first heard and now displeases as many—

They are gone, they are gone, the proud may lie by the proud.
Though we were bidden to sing, cry nothing loud.
They are gone, they are gone.
Whispering were enough.
Into the secret wilderness of their love.
A high, grey cairn. What more is to be said?
Eagles have gone into their cloudy bed.

The Green Helmet, an heroic farce, published in 1910, was originally written in prose, is based on the story of Bricriu's Feast, and is in rhyming Alexandrines which go very fast. The scene is a house on the sea-shore in orange,

89

red, black, purple colours; the open door showing the sea. When I saw the play years ago at the Abbey, the scene was so dark that we could hardly make out the shadowy figures. In lighting a comedy, if the scene is dark, one has to cheat. You establish the dimness and then bring up the lights discreetly. On that occasion the actors were unpractised in verse speaking and the rapid metre ran away with them so that a play which should have taken twenty or twenty-five minutes was over in thirteen—and we had scarcely heard a word of the gabble. It was the only occasion on which Yeats yielded to the heroic laughter and rough and tumble which you find in Bricriu's Feast and Mesca Uladh, the Intoxication of the Ulstermen. This play, which has never been staged in recent times, ends with a much admired passage, when the gigantic Red Man, who has dared the champions in turn to cut off his head, awards the National Prize—

> I have not come for your hurt, I'm the Rector of this land,
> And with my spitting cat-heads, my frenzied moon-bred band,
> Age after age I sift it, and choose for its championship
> The man who hits my fancy.

(*He places the Helmet on Cuchulain's head*)

> And I choose the laughing lip
> That shall not turn from laughing, whatever rise or fall;
> The heart that grows no bitterer although betrayed by all;
> The hand that loves to scatter; the life like a gambler's throw,
> And these things I make prosper, till a day come that I know,
> When heart and mind shall darken that the weak may end the strong,
> And the long-remembering harpers have matter for their song.

Professor Richard Ellman, who has written two books about Yeats, suggests that the early plays are really miracle plays. The young poet did suggest this when he was striving towards simplicity but I think he really meant Morality plays. In 1903 he wrote *The Hour Glass,* in which the pride of intellect is brought low, an uncharacteristic play, for Yeats had a fearless intellect. But he told us that it kept an alcoholic from drink for six months. Professor Ellmann also speaks of a mystical theatre, but when I saw these plays at the Abbey at the age of seventeen, I understood them, though I could not follow the poet's occult poetry.

In 1910 Yeats summed up his idea of the plays about which we have been speaking:

'The dignity of Greek drama, and in a lesser degree of that of Corneille and Racine, depends, as contrasted with the troubled life of Shakespearean drama, on an almost even speed of dialogue, and on a so continuous exclusion of the animation of common life, that thought remains lofty and language rich.'

Yeats could not read Corneille or Racine in French but, like George Moore, he got others to do his reading for him. The passage comes from an essay on Synge, who had been acclaimed as a great dramatist and in the essay—forgive me for saying it—I think Yeats was trying to suggest that Synge was writing the same sort of play as he did.

Yeats's Later Plays

Some time before W. B. Yeats went to live at Ballylee Tower, I met him for the first time. He was staying with his wife in a house opposite the main gate of Lady Gregory's domain. After lunch he talked to me about Donne and Landor, emphasised the need of discipline in verse, and then, much to my surprise, described how the Japanese, in their sacred processions, wore the grotesque masks and armour of their ancestors. I did not realise at the time that he had been studying the Noh plays which his friend, Ezra Pound, translated from the papers of the Italian scholar, Fenellosa, and that in these aristocratic ritual plays he had found a form in which he could express at last his own feeling for an art of dignified aloofness. Moreover here was a dramatic form in which he could also express his theosophical ideas and blend them with Irish myth. Owing to so much adverse criticism, he seems to have despaired of the stage and he returned to the literary salon or drawing-room in which such brief pieces could be played. The three Musicians who are narrators unfold a small curtain or cloth gravely and, when they fold it again, the actors are seen; no stage set is required. Unfortunately, the Victorian drawing-room was fast disappearing, and eventually Yeats had to put his Dance Plays on the stage. Meanwhile younger poets, like the mediaeval scholars, had returned to the taverns. Years later, Yeats heard of this and planned poetry recitals for the B.B.C., with a tavern as background. Being careful to get his facts right, he asked a young poet, the late F. R. Higgins, to bring him to a Dublin public house. There were the usual tobacco fumes and fellows calling out, 'Another pint of plain, Jim', or 'Two small ones, please'. After a few minutes, Yeats arose and said, 'Lead me out, Higgins, lead me out'.

The first Dance Play, *At the Hawk's Well*, 1917, has the

sparseness of his volume of poems, *Responsibilities,* 1914, and you will notice at once that the poet had to return to an old-fashioned type of description in following the Japanese originals to evoke the scene.

First Musician:

Night falls:
The mountain-side grows dark;
The withered leaves of the hazel
Half choke the dry bed of the well;
The guardian of the well is sitting
Upon the old grey stone at its side.

That mythic well which only fills for a few minutes at certain intervals is the mythic fountain of Everlasting Youth. Once more we have Cuchulain as a young man and an inevitable Old Man. The latter falls asleep and Cuchulain is beguiled from the spot, as the water returns, by the Hawk Dancer.

Mr. James McGarry, a member of the Committee of the Yeats Summer School at Sligo, showed me the rugged hill on the western side of the Ox Mountains, which is known as the Hawk's Rock. At the summit there is a well which rises and falls daily with the near-by tide. He was certain that Yeats must have been thinking of this well when he wrote his Dance Play, for he had often strayed among those mountains in his youthful days.

The second Dance Play was *The Only Jealousy of Emer,* 1919. When the Lyric Theatre Company revived this Dance Play on the Abbey stage, one of our problems was that the Woman of the Sidhe had to dance and speak verse at the same time. Our producer solved the problem by giving the verse to one of the Narrators, while the Dancer mimed to the words. We undertook some of the Dance Plays because Anne Yeats, who designed the sets for us, had found in a damp cellar of the Abbey the magnificent masks designed by Edmund Dulac—thrown aside in a corner. In the Noh plays Yeats had found much that he wanted: spirits, ghosts, demonic possession. Bricriu of the Bitter Tongue

93

assumes the body of the stricken Cuchulain and speaks in a mediumistic way. Cuchulain's wife, Emer, and his mistress, Eithne Inguba, are by the bedside and it is noticeable here how Yeats leaves his new stark style at times and returns to a rich romantic music, as when Emer says—

No, not yet, for first
I'll cover up his face to hide the sea;
And throw new logs upon the hearth and stir
The half-burnt logs until they break in flame.
Old Manannan's unbridled horses come
Out of the sea, and on their backs his horsemen;
But all the enchantments of the dreaming foam
Dread the hearth-fire.

Bricrui, the enemy of Fand, the Sidhe woman, tells Emer that there is only one way of saving her husband, by relinquishing him to his mistress—a highly dramatic climax.

Figure of Cuchulain:
There is still a moment left; cry out, cry out!
Renounce him, and her power is at an end.
Cuchulain's foot is on the chariot-step.
Cry—

Emer:
I renounce Cuchulain's love for ever.

It is noticeable I think that in this play Yeats uses attractively and romantically those phases of the moon which he was to elaborate in *A Vision* and rarely succeeded in using effectively in his poems—

Ghost of Cuchulain:
Who is it stands before me there
Shedding such light from limb and hair
As when the moon, complete at last
With every labouring crescent past,
And lonely with extreme delight,
Flings out upon the fifteenth night?

He is, of course, speaking to Fand.

I have mislaid my copy of Fenellosa but I remember noticing that the theme of *The Dreaming of the Bones*

94

1919, was based on a Japanese plot and this may apply less closely to the other three Dance Plays. Here the evoked setting is contemporary. A young volunteer, 'on the run' after 1916 in north Clare near the Abbey of Corcomroe at night, meets a stranger and a young girl in the costume of a past time, wearing heroic masks. They are Diarmuid and Dervorgilla but no longer middle-aged. They must wander until someone of our race forgives them. When the Young Man guesses the identity of these phantoms, he refuses the forgiveness. A recent American critic, Mrs. Helen Hennessy Vendler, writes:

> 'The main difficulty with *The Dreaming of the Bones* is that there is no necessary connection between the lovers and the young man'.

—although he tells us that they had brought the Normans in. I do not think, despite the Hennessy, that Mrs. Vendler knows much about Irish history.

When I first went to London, I stayed in a cheap lodging house and when we were having our nourishing meals in the kitchen, the workmen often complained about a neighbour who kept cockerels, as the crowing woke them up at drawn. I dared not tell them that when I was wakened at cockcrow, I thought of some lines in this play of Yeats and was on my way back to Ireland. Listen to the words of the much-abused King Diarmuid—

This pathway
Runs to the ruined Abbey of Corcomroe;
The Abbey passed, we are soon among the stone
And shall be at the ridge before the cocks
Of Aughanish or Bailevelehan
Or grey Aughtmana shake their wings and cry.

And the play ends, as I reminded you previously, with a lyric about music of a lost kingdom, of which the last stanza begins—

My heart ran wild when it heard
The curlew cry before dawn

95

And the eddying cat-headed bird—

Yeats's oft-repeated description of the owl.

Curiously enough in 1922 Yeats returned to the stage with a play in the ordinary European technique written in imaginative prose. Although not called so, *The Player Queen* is really a comedy with an ironic turn, in two scenes or acts, one short, one long, and it takes a little over an hour to play in the theatre. In the background is the familiar mediaeval symbol which Yeats has used before, the unicorn, which can only be tamed by a virgin. A band of strolling players, like those met by Hamlet, come to a more respectable Elsinore at a time of political crisis. The people are murmuring and the Regent or Prime Minister as he is called, is worried for the young queen, who has never known the world and has lived in her palace unseen, refuses to come out on the balcony. During a rehearsal of the strolling players, the Prime Minister sees Decima, the lively and attractive leading lady of the troupe. The queen has been anxious to retire to a convent and he suddenly finds the political solution. The people have never seen her and, with her permission, he presents Decima in royal robes before the crowd as their queen—and incidentally marries her. Except for the grief of the drunken poet Septimus, whom Decima refused to marry, all ends happily. But not according to Professor T. R. Henn, who, in his book, *The Harvest of Tragedy*, regards this play as a tragedy and writes:

'It is unique among tragedies in that it represents the triumph of pure evil, and the destruction by woman (who takes her sexual revenge upon him, and by society), of the inspired poet. It is difficult to read and more difficult to act: when both difficulties are overcome the play acquires a strange and sinister life of its own'.

The Cat and the Moon, 1926, is in prose but has, as in the Noh plays, an opening and concluding lyric, both about Minnaloushe, the cat. And here again the astrological imagery is used lyrically:—

96

Does Minnaloushe know that his pupils
Will pass from change to change,
And that from round to crescent,
From crescent to round they range?
Minnaloushe creeps through the grass
Alone, important and wise,
And lifts to the changing moon
His changing eyes.

This is an inimical satire on George Moore. Edward
Martyn wrote a more kindly one for his rival theatre in
Hardwick Street, which presented only non-folk realistic
plays. On the opening night of his satiric play most
of us did not know what it was all about, but the
author sat in front laughing at his own jokes on the stage.
By the way, Minnaloushe, a beautiful cat which Maud
Gonne owned, met with a terrible death. It was sleeping
in an electric oven and someone switched on the current.

Calvary (1920) and *The Resurrection* (1931) were not
produced at the Abbey as far as I know. Of the latter, the
author wrote: 'Before I had finished this play I saw that
its subject-matter might make it unsuitable for the public
stage in England or in Ireland.' In England there were
certain legal restrictions regarding scriptural plays, and
here there was public opinion. Both plays are based on the
Alexandrian school of neo-Platonism. The theme of 'Calvary', which is partly in prose, partly in verse, is expressed
in the words of Judas—

Is there a secret left I do not know,
Knowing that if a man betrays a God
He is the stronger of the two?

The Resurrection begins with a famous lyric which owes
something to Shelley—

Another Troy must rise and set,
Another lineage feed the crow,
Another Argo's painted prow
Drive to a flashier bauble yet.

and ends with the much quoted line—

97

Whatever flames upon the night
Man's own resinous heart has fed.

The play takes place on the feast of Dionysius and at times
the religious revellers cross the stage. It is mainly a theo-
logical debate between a Hebrew, a Syrian and a Greek.
Yeats objected to Maud Gonne indulging in argument but
here he does it himself, and very effectively. I saw the two
plays when they were presented for the first time by the
Trinity Players a few years ago and was surprised by their
stage effectiveness as I had only read them. And there may
be a moral in this, namely, that one should see a play
before judging it. The play reminded me of two by Euripi-
des, 'The Bacchantes' and his 'Helene', in which a phantom
of Helen is welcomed in Egypt, while the real Helen remains entranced in Asia Minor.

The very short play, *A Full Moon in March,* published
in 1935, is in the Noh form but the re-written version, *The
King of the Great Clock Tower,* which appeared the same
year, has no preparatory lyric. Here we have a Gaelic
legend used in an early prose tale by the poet and slightly
touched by the *Fin de Siècle* play of Oscar Wilde, *Salome.*
Yeats had become interested in decapitation, a subject
known to Freudians. Let us pass on hastily to *Purgatory,*
a play in which, according to T. S. Eliot, Yeats became for
the first time a dramatist. Here Yeats abandoned the Noh
form and we have the usual stage-set. The theme, according
to some critics, expresses his later aristocratic attitude as it
deals with the dire consequences of a marriage between
high and low. The aged man in the play was the son of a
groom in a racing stable who had married a wealthy lady.
Ill-treated by his father, he killed him and became
a wanderer. The theme has some resemblance to *The
Dreaming of the Bones:* his parents must work out
their penance by reliving their past life. An upper window
of the ruined house lights up and the ghost of the father is
seen. In the first Abbey production, a very substantial
ghost appeared drinking from a real bottle of Power's or

Jameson's. Nowadays this scene is played with a bare stage with lighting off-stage to suggest the window. Against current critical opinion, I find the play unpleasant: patricide and filocide all in one short act is too much: and I still wonder why the hefty young son in the play did not even struggle when his father was getting rid of him. The style is as bare as the set should be and the factual lines show a new development of detail—

> Great people lived and died in this house;
> Magistrates, colonels, members of Parliament,
> Captains and Governors, and long ago
> Men that had fought at Aughrim and the Boyne.
> Some that had gone on Government work
> To London or to India came home to die,
> Or came from London every spring.

This brings up an interesting point: Yeats's description of the contemporary world had always been selective. He made many lecture tours to the United States but the only reference to that country is a line in the poem 'His Phoenix'—

> And there's a player in the States...

Much of his youth was spent in London but, apart from a reference to the Cheshire Cheese, we have only a line in a late poem about a tea-shop there. This of course was the flight of the last romantics. The production of *Purgatory* caused a row at the time. An eminent Jesuit claimed that the poet had no right to use as his title the word 'purgatory', which primarily refers to a specific Catholic doctrine. At a subsequent public meeting the manager of the Abbey, the late F. R. Higgins, who was not a theologian, was badly routed.

Moving past that prose play, *The Words upon the Window Pane*, which ends with a very dramatic line spoken by the medium in the tone of Swift, we come to the last two plays, which were published posthumously: *The Herne's Egg* and *The Death of Cuchulain*. Both remained unproduced in the theatre which the poet had founded and

99

the Lyric Theatre Company had the honour of giving them on that stage their world premières—though the world took no notice of us. In the middle of the rehearsals of *The Herne's Egg* we heard that the Third Programme of the B.B.C. was about to produce it and I wrote to the late Louis MacNeice, who agreed very kindly to postpone the broadcast. Later some higher authority must have glanced at the play and decided that it was not for the pure ears of the British public and so it was never broadcast. We had solved that problem by not emphasising the complex images which might have been found offensive to good taste and so there was not the usual riot at the performance. *The Herne's Egg* is a madcap Rabelaisian extravaganza with a smiling pantomimic moon on the backcloth. For the theme Yeats went back to Ferguson's long poem, 'Congal', which he had read in his youth. The egg laid was in fact a goose egg and by an unfortunate mistake was served in a wooden dish to the King while his lessers were given dishes of silver. The inner theme is again a favourite one of Yeats, that of re-incarnation. Yeats increases the insult—

I have had a common egg,
A common hen's egg put before me,
An egg dropped in the dirty straw
And crowed for by a cross-bred gangling cock,
And every other man at the table
A herne's egg.

The King is slain by a fool at the wrong moment for transmigration and becomes in his new life a donkey.

In the very short play, *The Death of Cuchulain* I feel that Yeats was working out a very personal kind of drama for himself. He had begun with a poem on the death of Cuchulain fifty years before, and this theme reaches a highly imaginative intensity here. It starts with the vivid Prologue which I have mentioned before, spoken by the Old Man, 'looking like something out of mythology'. The Old Man and the Blind Man, as mentioned in the stage directions, step out of the play, *On Baile's Strand.* The Morrigu or War Goddess arranges a dance—the only trace of the Japanese convention left in this play, except in the closing lyric, in which we are suddenly transferred to the twentieth century. The accompaniment is pipe-and-drum music. We used a tin whistle and borrowed the drum from the band of the Transport Workers' Union—I think Yeats would have been pleased by that. The place in the G.P.O. where the statue of Cuchulain now stands, is indicated in the last lines of the song.

Purgatory was written in octosyllabic measure, but *The Death of Cuchulain* is in blank verse, although T. S. Eliot has laid it down that this metrical form is out of date. A metrical note, therefore, may be necessary. Stage speech only resembles natural speech, and the trained actor finds it easier to speak than ordinary prose owing to its pattern. In metrical verse there cannot be more than three syllables between each accent; when the primary accents are skilfully played against the light ones so that they are hardly heard, the paragraphic run-ons can suggest contemporary speech rhythm. I may mention that octosyllabic measure can sound slower than it looks because of the shorter time-space between the pauses at the end of the line. In his later dramas Eliot used a line with three or four shifting accents. Owing to the difficulty of scanning, actors tend to speak the verse as though it were prose.

A very useful booklet appeared a few years ago from the Dolmen Press, *Yeats and the Noh: Types of Japanese Beauty and their Reflection in Yeats's Plays,* by Hiro Ishibashi, edited by Anthony Kerrigan. One of the differences between Yeats and the Noh is that Yeats did not subordinate all the elements of his plays to the prominence of the Main Player. Influenced by the overtly original translations of Noh plays by Fenellosa-Pound, Yeats failed to recognise the importance given the Main Player in the Japanese original. The drama in Yeats's plays most typically develops between two conflicting characters. Yeats was well

101

aware of the beauty inherent in the attitude of the warrior class of Japan in the Middle Ages. One of his favourite possessions was a Japanese sword, which he felt was a symbol of his soul, in the manner of the Japanese warriors —a terrible beauty!

The Dreaming of the Bones is known to be modelled on *Nishikigi*. In the Japanese Dreaming-back, as it is called, it is in the dream of the Main Player that the dead appear. *At the Hawk's Well* is based on the Noh play, *Izutsu* or *The Well*. In the strict Noh form, the Hawk would have been the Main Player, who normally chants and dances the most beautiful part in Noh plays.

During the last three decades of the nineteenth century the range of prose drama developed in remarkable ways. Ibsen moved from realism towards a symbolic method in his final phase. Strindberg abandoned his stark naturalism and wrote a number of short plays — among them *The Spook Sonata* — during his Blue Tower period, and they were to have much influence in the new century. The Blue Tower was the name of a small theatre given to the Swedish dramatist by a few of his friends, and it can be regarded as the precursor of the Little Theatres which were to give shelter to experimental drama. The social dramas of Ibsen influenced Bernard Shaw in his revolt from Victorian convention and, despite critical opposition, he succeeded in proving that plays in which the pro's and con's of argument are more important than characters can hold interest. In order to attract pit and gallery, Shaw occasionally compromised and used well-worn plots, which he cleverly reversed for polemic purposes. The plot, for example, of *Arms and the Man* was pirated abroad, suffered a sea-change and appeared as a light opera called *The Chocolate Soldier*. Despite his annoyance, Shaw did not profit from this commercial ingenuity and so the worst was to come. Shortly after his death, one of his most popular plays, *Pygmalion*, was exploited, complete with happy ending, in a sentimental Musical, *My Fair Lady*.

Shaw was also influenced by Chekhov and paid tribute to the Russion dramatist in *Heartbreak House*. In adapting the unresolved ending used by Chekhov in such plays as *The Cherry Orchard* and *The Three Sisters*, Shaw moved from the conventional tragedy of the past to the new drama of reality. Unfortunately the busy Chekhov was not fully aware of his own discovery and in some of his best-known plays he returned to the tragic convention; too often the distraught hero rushes off and, with a crack of a hasty pistol, the curtain descends.

The simple and repetitive phrases which Maeterlinck used in his subjective tragedies to express the spiritual plight of his characters were, after undue neglect, to have a surprising influence on contemporary experimental drama in England and France. Harold Pinter, for example, uses this device in his dialogue, in order to emphasise the ordinariness of his characters.

Recent critics have pointed out that the later plays of Strindberg inspired German expressionistic drama, which spread rapidly after the first Great War. The plays of Ernst Toller, Georg Kaiser and others were rhythmic in movement and poetic in tone. I hasten to add, however, that this new method was anticipated in the nineties by Gerhart Hauptmann in his subjective play, *Hannele*. *The Old Lady says 'No'*, by Denis Johnston is an Irish example of Expressionism, and, in two plays, *The Hairy Ape* and *Emperor Jones, the Irish-American dramatist*, Eugene O'Neill has given us exciting examples. In France the belated influence of Strindberg is shown in Cocteau's play, *Orphée*, which was designed to express poetry in and by action.

The psychological drama of Pirandello has also widened the scope of the stage but his example has not been followed to any extent. Unfortunately he yielded at times to the dire tragic ending and that much-admired play, *Henry IV*, ends with an unexpected display of theatrical violence. The 'epic' plays of Berthold Brecht have attracted

103

much interest despite their naïve expression of necessary social reforms. *Mother Courage* was intended by the author as a satiric depiction of a shrewd vivandière, but audiences seized on the comprehensive title and reacted instantly to the deeply moving, episodic account of the Thirty Years' War.

Liberty has been gained by prose dramatists but the verse dramatist who endeavours to pass beyond the pseudo-Elizabethan barrier, of which Yeats was aware only in a vague way, must continue to meet with prejudice. Modern verse plays are produced seldom; even in Little Theatres, audiences are inclined to dislike an experience to which they are unaccustomed. The critical disparagement of the lyric plays of Yeats may be summarised in a patronising sentence by Edmund Wilson: 'Yeats's plays have little dramatic importance because Yeats himself has little sense of drama, and we think of them primarily as a department of his poetry, with the same sort of interest and beauty as the rest.' For more than fifty years Yeats continued to write verse dramas for the stage and his devotion cannot be disregarded. Even critics as unsympathetic as Edmund Wilson admit that his long years in the theatre eventually gave dramatic force to his later poems. My personal regret is that the poet chose to write some plays in prose, such as *The Player Queen*, *The Resurrection* and *The Words upon the Window-Pane*. I have endeavoured in the foregoing talks to trace his development from *The Countess Cathleen* and the middle plays to the Dance Plays with their symbolic movement and that last experiment, in elliptical scenes, *The Death of Cuchulain*. Let me end with another sentence by Edmund Wilson from his essay in *Axel's Castle* on the work of the Irish poet: 'The Abbey Theatre has taken a Naturalistic turn which Yeats never contemplated or desired; but his long and uncompromising campaign for a revival of poetic drama contributed much to contemporary efforts to break up the rigid technique and clear the stage of the realistic encumbrances of the Naturalistic drama.'